SIMPLICITY

STRATEGIC PLANNING
FOR BUSINESS AND LIFE

BRIAN J. RHINESS

Order this book online at www.trafford.com
or email orders@trafford.com

Most Trafford titles are also available at major online book retailers.

Printed in the United States of America.

ISBN: 978-1-4907-3579-5 (sc)
ISBN: 978-1-4907-3580-1 (hc)
ISBN: 978-1-4907-3581-8 (e)

Library of Congress Control Number: 2014909035

Trafford rev. 05/27/2014

www.trafford.com
North America & international
toll-free: 1 888 232 4444 (USA & Canada)
fax: 812 355 4082

To all those with the relentless curiosity to learn and grow.

CONTENTS

Section 3: Execution

INTRODUCTION

Why Write This Book?

I must start with a confession: I do not like strategic planning. My preference is to get busy making things happen. Getting results is much more exciting and rewarding.

After many years of leading organizations and serving on boards I have participated in countless strategic planning exercises. Some were worthwhile and successful, most were not. It would have been easy to conclude that strategic planning is a waste of time. That knee jerk reaction conflicted with my firm belief that setting and implementing strategic direction is the number one role of leaders and vital to the future of any organization. An organization without a plan will not achieve its potential and will be in constant danger of total failure. My response to this dilemma was to set up a strategic advisory company and use my hard learned lessons to help make the planning process simpler and more successful for leading individuals and organizations. The Rhiness Group was born.

The foundation of The Rhiness Group and this book is to make strategic planning and execution simple. Simple is not the same as easy. Much of the work that comes out of strategic planning exercises will be hard. It can take years of effort to successfully implement strategies and get the results you are looking for. What should be simple and clear is the direction you are taking and the actions needed to get you there. Throughout this book you will be constantly reminded of The Rhiness Group motto:

Simplicity—Clarity—Action—Results

It is not just a motto but a proven way of doing strategic planning that makes the process less painful and dramatically improves your chances of success. Throughout the book we will stress keeping things simple and clear. People like to take action on things and they want to get results. You want your people to do exactly that. If you are giving them complex and confusing direction, they will take action and you will get results. Will they be the actions and results you want? You will get much better results if your directions are simple and clear and lead to measureable results.

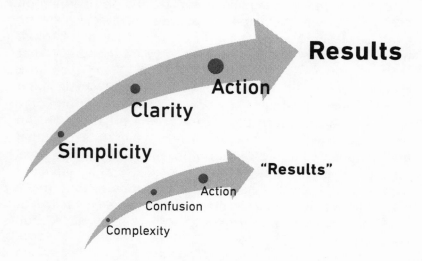

It is a well documented fact that more than 75% of strategic plans fail. They fail for a number of reasons.

In many cases the plan is developed by a small group of senior managers at their annual planning event (sometimes linked to a recreational opportunity) and then placed in a desk somewhere until it is brought out for review the following year. It was never intended to be implemented. In other cases people are serious about building a real plan but fail to involve the right people so there is no buy-in and implementation fails. Still others will hire a high priced outside organization to create the plan and deliver it to them with great fanfare. These are the biggest, brightest and most costly flameouts.

There is no shortcut to successful strategic planning. It absolutely requires full support and commitment from the senior ranks of the organization. You will need to involve as many stakeholders as possible to ensure buy-in and then unwavering focus on daily execution of the plan. If that sounds like hard work, it is. Anything worthwhile, like your organization or your life plan, requires commitment and hard work. This book will show you how to make the **process** of planning and implementing simple and straightforward.

Effective strategic planning and implementation requires the commitment and direct involvement of everyone in the organization. It is highly advisable to bring in an outside facilitator. Even in cases where you have very good strategic planning people on staff, you will benefit from outside help. An outside facilitator can act as a guide and remove process issues that can be a barrier to what you are really seeking—a great conversation. Internal people, no matter how great, will always bring a bias to the process. Look for that trusted advisor to be your guide.

I talk to a lot of people about strategic planning. In some cases, I turn down potential contracts when it is obvious the people are not serious, are looking for easy answers or are doing it because a lender, board or partner are demanding it. There are also senior managers that will emphatically state that they do not need a plan, they are solely focussed on execution. **_Executing what?_** Without a plan there is nothing real to execute. People in those organizations are confused and frustrated. They show up for work every day wanting to do something that makes a difference with no hope. Execution without a visible plan is pure folly.

Strategic planning is not an event; it is an on-going process. What that really means is that you must commit yourself and the organization to _strategic management_. Strategic management is the plan, effective implementation and sustaining high performance on an on-going basis. In this book we will take you through the steps to turn that plan on the shelf into a living process.

Effective strategic management brings with it the clarity, the accountability, the trust and the focus needed to dramatically improve your chances of success.

This book will guide you through the steps of effective strategic management for your organization. There is no one process or magic formula that works for all organizations. If someone tells you they have a template strategic planning process that works for everyone, show them the door quickly. You and your organization are unique. The process must be suited for your organization. We will show you how to do that. The steps in this book can be used for building your personal life plan as well. Look for the section on building your life plan (p. 77).

We have designed the book to be user friendly. You can go back at anytime and check specific sections, go over the key questions to ask or just help get things back on track.

Many organizations fear that keeping things simple makes them appear unsophisticated or uninteresting. A complex plan better reflects how complex their business is. This is absolutely wrong. Who are you trying to impress? Most organizations are doing complex things and yours is no exception. Successful organizations have clear strategic priorities that everyone can focus on.

Some advisory companies will try to saddle you with long, drawn out processes and extravagant models. They will deliver documents that no one can interpret. If you cannot explain it, you cannot implement it. Allow me to guide you from complexity to the beauty of simplicity and better results.

At the start of this chapter I admitted that I do not like strategic planning. I do have a passion for helping individuals and organizations succeed. This book comes from that passion and my commitment to help you in your journey. Enjoy the read.

Brian J. Rhiness

HOW TO USE THIS BOOK

It is not necessary to be an expert on strategic planning to build and implement a great plan. If you are reading this book to assist in building a new life plan, all of the building blocks are here to help you change your life. If you are part of an organization that does not have a strategic plan, or has a plan that is not working, you now have a user's manual to guide you step by step to a simple, clear plan that will drive the actions needed to get the results you desire.

The book begins with the foundations of planning. There is no "one size fits all" strategic plan, sufficient for every organization and every circumstance. You and your organization are unique and your current circumstances are unique. Therefore your plan must be unique, fitted to your organization and no other. Start with Getting Ready to Plan (p. 3). Understanding where you are and the basics of planning will save you time and ensure your plan is right for you.

The book will be especially helpful as a resource manual for those working in organizations that have just begun the process of strategic planning. In section two, we show you each critical step necessary to get the most out of your planning process (p. 35). We always recommend bringing in outside help to guide you in the process and this section gives you the knowledge to ask the right questions of any potential guide. The best strategic plans come from the best conversations. We show you how to ensure you have the right conversation with the right people.

At the end of each chapter is a list of Simplicity Keys. These are the most important questions, ideas, and concepts from that chapter. Use the Simplicity Keys as a quick reminder as you move through your own planning process.

This is an action oriented book and section three takes you through execution (p. 85). Execution is where most plans fail. We show you what to watch out for, how to ensure real accountability and give you the tools to improve your implementation success.

Even the best strategic plans struggle, stall or go completely off the tracks. Expect it and use it as an opportunity to kick start the plan and the strategic priorities that have been set (p. 114). Remember, the best plans take time, focus and regular updating. We show you proven ways to turn your plan into results.

This book does not answer all of questions around strategic planning. It is a practical, user friendly guide to help you build a plan that works. Keep it handy and refer back to it regularly to get on track and stay on track.

If you have questions, contact us through our web site: www.RhinessGroup.com. We are always happy to assist with your planning process. The web site also includes articles and other information that will be helpful in your journey.

SECTION 1

GETTING READY TO PLAN

CHAPTER 1

Getting Ready to Plan

"In preparing for battle I have always found that plans are useless, but planning is indispensible"
—Dwight D. Eisenhower

Do not jump right into planning. Many try the old standard of pulling a few people into a room (sometimes on a weekend) and whipping a plan together. That never works.

As a leader, you must show that you have a clear picture of what you wish to achieve with a planning process. Take the time to understand what you are looking for and how it should proceed. A little extra time at the start will save time down the road and improve the chances of building and implementing a successful plan. By taking time, we do not mean months or years. If someone suggests to you that it will take that long, they are misleading you. We have successfully completed planning processes with organizations in a few shorts weeks using the techniques we will cover in this book.

Stop.

Ask the right questions.

Then proceed in a manner that will build confidence with those involved from the very start. Hours spent at the start of planning will save weeks down the road.

This first section of the book will help you understand what you are looking for in a strategic plan, the steps you will go through and how you will do it. Take the time to read the chapters on strategic leadership (p. 7), systems thinking (p. 11) and strategic management (p. 24). This is the foundation of a great planning process.

Strategic planning is personal. It is personal for you and everyone in the organization. We do not believe in standard templates that some companies say fit all organizations. They do not work. Other organizations can have a strategic plan very similar to yours. You must start with the attitude of *"what will make ours' different?"* Every organization is unique. Strategic planning is about the *conversation,* not a fill in the blanks template. Build a process that ensures the right conversation and you will come out with a plan that works for your organization. This book is designed to help guide you through that conversation.

As you read through the first section of the book, keep these questions in the back of your mind:

- Do we have an existing plan?
- Have we actually attempted to implement that plan?
- Is that plan working?
- Will we be adjusting a plan or starting from scratch?
- What kind of outside help do we need?
- What kind of process will we use?
- What is the timeline to get this done?
- What resources will we need?
- How will we get the results we need?
- What will make our plan different?

We always recommend bringing in outside help to facilitate the planning process. A good facilitator will remove the burden of the process and allow participants to focus on the conversation and the content. They will also remove the perception of bias that can prevent the open and honest conversation that is the foundation of the great strategic plan.

If you have decided to use outside help in guiding you through the process, bring them into the discussion as early as possible. Ask questions of them and ensure that what they are recommending meets your needs. We are often asked if a group should find a facilitator that is an expert in the groups' industry. If you can find someone, it may be helpful. They will come with a basic understanding of the industry language and the learning curve is not quite as steep. The other side of the argument, which is equally valid, is that someone without industry knowledge brings no bias and will not insert any bias into the conversation. Look for a good facilitator first and if they have some industry knowledge that is a bonus.

To find the right facilitator, ask other organizations who they have used and if they are happy with the results. Those organizations can be in totally different industries or other jurisdictions. Ask them:

1. Did the facilitator keep the process in the background and focus on the conversation?
2. Did the facilitator's style work for your organization?
3. Did you get the results you were looking for?
4. Would you use the person again?

When you have identified some potential facilitators, ask them those questions you have been keeping in the back of your mind. They should be able to quickly lay out a recommended process based on your needs. Beware of sales pitches. An effective planning process will have some bumps and a good facilitator will not avoid them, but instead embrace and use them for better results. If you are promised a smooth ride, move to the next name on the list. You are looking for the person that can pull the best ideas from the passionate people in your organization. That means it is going to be a bumpy ride. The best facilitators enjoy bringing that passion to the surface.

Before you sign a contract with a facilitator, test that person with the senior management in the organization. The key relationship in the planning process is between the senior people that are responsible for the strategic plan and the facilitator. There must be both comfort and trust. The test can be a simple as a telephone conversation to discuss the basics of the planning process. You are opening the lines of communication that will be critical as you move through the planning and implementation phases. Take the time to get the right people in place. This is a theme which you will be reminded of throughout the book.

A final caution: never turn the creation or writing of your strategic plan over to someone outside the organization. Assign one individual in your group to work directly with the facilitator on the results from all planning discussions. Even if you have a planning team, one person should be assigned as the lead contact. That person keeps possession of all flip charts, summaries, surveys and other materials. They will work with the facilitator on the draft documents that will be prepared for approval and implementation.

Simplicity Keys

> Determine the kind of process that you need.
> Make sure the plan is unique to your organization
> Find a good, recommended outside facilitator to guide you through the process
> Never turn the creation or writing of your strategic plan over to someone outside your organization

CHAPTER 2

Strategic Leadership

*"Leadership means bringing people
together in pursuit of a common cause,
developing a plan to achieve it and staying
with it until the goal is achieved"*
—Bill Clinton

Leadership is not easy. Even those individuals that have been recognized as great leaders will quickly admit that they are still trying to get it right. That is probably why they are great leaders. They are still working at it and know they will never get there.

The section on strategic leadership is near the start of the book because without someone taking the responsibility for strategic planning and implementation it will never get done. In most cases, this person must be the CEO of the organization but as you will see it can be anyone in a leadership role of a work unit or group. Many of the tasks can be delegated to a planning team, but the responsibility stays with the leader. There are cases where a board of directors will push for a strategic plan to be completed. The board has a vital role in the process and must be fully involved. However, without the CEO who is responsible for implementation on side the plan is lost and the planning process is a waste of time. If the CEO is unwilling to undertake a real strategic planning process with every intention of full commitment to implementation, the board has a more important decision to make first.

The three basic responsibilities of a leader are:

- Strategic—setting the direction for the organization
- Execution—implementing, monitoring, adjusting and getting it done
- Development—building the people, capabilities, capacity and culture

If any of these three roles are lacking, the leader will not achieve their full potential. There is no question that some people are better at some things than others. The best leaders recognize their weak areas and surround themselves with people that fill in the gaps. The great leader is really a team of highly effective people. There is no differentiation between leaders and managers. You must be both. It is a myth that a great leader can do the "vision thing" and somehow it magically gets done. The "vision thing" is followed by a lot of hard work on execution and building the people, culture and capacity to achieve the desired results.

Strategic Leadership takes it up a notch. The strategic leader must be able to take the critical and at times complex issues and potential solutions facing the organization and translate them into simple, clear messages that all stakeholders can understand. The strategic leader stays obsessively focused on the vision that has been set and can answer that important question "what is in it for me?" for each and every stakeholder. The strategic leader delivers real results while always honoring the values of the organization.

A strategic leader sets the tone for the organization they lead. Strategic leadership can happen at any level in an organization. You do not have to be the CEO to be a strategic leader. You do not even need people reporting to you. If we go back to the three basic responsibilities of a leader, we can replace the word organization with project, initiative, life or whatever fits where you are today. The same steps apply. As you go through the book, look for how the steps apply to where you are today and begin using them every day. The results will be profound.

Some middle managers respond that there is no corporate strategic plan; so how can they have a plan for their work unit? Easy. Just go ahead and build one using the principles in this book. When others in the organization see the results you are getting they will eventually follow. Leadership can come from anywhere. It can also be a great idea to test run strategic planning in smaller work units before doing the overall corporate plan. We will talk later about integrating plans throughout the organization.

In your work unit, you can start setting the tone of strategic leadership by demonstrating on a day to day basis a few basic traits. Try these tomorrow and build on them each day until they become the way you do business:

- Be the best you can in your current role
- Step up—if you have a vision, share it and push it
- Be willing to evolve and be patient with yourself and others
- Encourage ideas from everyone in the group
- Embrace skeptics—they are your best friends
- Always have your staffs' backs
- Accept responsibility for mistakes and admit them quickly
- Avoid "yes" people
- Allow no hidden agendas
- Show clarity of purpose—keep testing with stakeholders
- Monitor your progress—measure the important stuff
- Ask for and use feedback from all stakeholders

- Stretch the group to achieve great things—if everyone is comfortable you are not trying hard enough
- Manage all aspects of your work unit—the small stuff is the big stuff

Some believe that to be a strategic thinker you must be a "big picture" thinker. That may help but it is not essential. If in managing your current work unit, you can see how it fits and supports the entire organization and you can lead your group in fulfilling the potential of the organization, you are a strategic leader.

If your first reaction is that leadership is not for me, stop for a minute. Leadership and management are not for everyone. We all know people that should never have been in a leadership role. This is personal to you. Answer these questions and pick the spots that work best for you:

- Is being more effective in your current job important?
- Do you want to be happier in your life and relationships?
- Do you want to make a larger contribution in your community?

Following the principles in this book will help you in any aspect of your life and career. We need you to take on that strategic leadership role before we can be successful in planning and execution. Without you it will not get done.

Simplicity Keys

➢ The three basic responsibilities of a leader are: strategic, execution and development
➢ Remember that leadership can come from anywhere in the organization
➢ Decide if you really want to be a leader/manager
➢ Demonstrate the traits of a strategic leader every day
➢ Answer "what's in it for me?" for all stakeholders

CHAPTER 3

Systems Thinking Simplicity

"If life on earth is governed by the natural laws of living systems, then a successful participant should learn the rules"
—Stephen G. Haines

What is systems thinking?

Systems thinking is a holistic approach that views the whole as being primary and the parts as secondary. It focuses on the relationships between the parts rather than the individual parts themselves. Systems thinking is based on *general systems theory*, a field of study pioneered by Ludwig von Bertalanffy in the 1950s. By using systems thinking you will see the interdependencies, connections and cycles in any problem. In linear thinking these relationships are ignored and focus is only on the solution with no consideration of possible consequences.

A system is a set of pieces that work together for the benefit of the whole. Our bodies are a system. As individuals we are a living system and part of larger systems such as communities, countries and planet Earth.

Each system is made up of interrelated pieces that will have an effect on the functioning of the whole. Each of the pieces will affect other pieces in the system. The whole system will have characteristics that none of the individual pieces possess.

Lead by example

Your organization is a system. It is a collection of individual units or tasks that function to benefit the organization as a whole. We know from experience that if something goes wrong in one part of the organization, it will have an effect on the other parts. It is for this reason that systems thinking is the very best foundation for planning, execution and on-going operations.

We like to use the visual of the helicopter. Getting up above of the ground level and day to day issues to see what is really going on. What does the whole system/ operation look like? How are different pieces affecting each other? What is really going on in the organization beyond each individual division's problems? Leaders at all levels in the organization need to lead by example and show they are focussed on the entire operation. Boards and senior management teams should use systems thinking in building their strategic and execution plans.

A simple illustration of a system model: Systems Thinking Simplicity

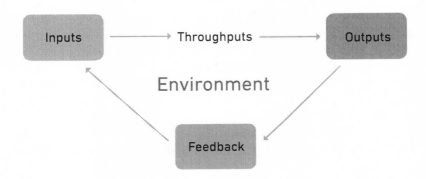

Any living system has inputs, outputs, throughputs, feedback on how things are working and it operates in an environment. All of the pieces are vital to the healthy functioning of the system. If anything is missing, we have system failure.

Look at any manufacturing process. We have the output of a product which we plan to sell. We have inputs including parts, a factory, machinery and staff. Throughputs include the actual manufacturing steps that result in a finished product. Feedback tells us how we are doing and can be measured in units/hour, defects, profit/unit and anything else deemed important. We also exist in an environment which includes our marketplace, economy, country, global competition, supplier network and customer base. This is a very complex mix of factors that can mean success or failure for our business.

We can bring the beauty of simplicity to this complex mix by going back to the model. While some of the technology, measures and marketing efforts may be very complex, why we are doing them and where they fit is not. Everything can be classed as an input, an output, a feedback, or an element of the environment. By constantly going back to the systems model we can maintain focus on what is important.

Stephen Covey, in his great book <u>The Seven Habits of Highly Successful People</u> talks about *beginning with the end in mind*. This is systems thinking. He is referring to the focus on outputs/outcomes and the need to start there. Our feedback measures will be matched to the results we wish to achieve. Inputs will be adjusted as necessary to support those outcomes. Throughputs will take those inputs and give us the outputs we desire. At all times we must be aware of the environment we operate in and what is changing.

You can see the linkages. If we start with the wrong desired outputs/outcomes it is impossible to put the right measures, inputs and throughputs in place to be successful. If we do have the right outputs/outcomes but do not measure the right things, we will not know how we are doing. If we have the right outputs/outcomes and measures in place and our inputs do not support those, we will fail. The system is a cycle where all pieces must support each other. One weak link destroys the system.

For more effective strategic planning and management we have taken the systems thinking model and developed Strategic Thinking Simplicity. This simple approach to planning and execution provides your organization with the clarity needed undertake the right actions to give you the desired results you are looking for.

Systems Thinking is different from analytical thinking. Analytical thinking will focus on a problem and potential solutions without consideration for the whole system. This leads to "unintended consequences" that will negatively affect the organization. In strategic planning we need both systems thinking and analytical thinking. Start with a systems thinking approach and the big picture and when you get to execution utilize analytical thinking to build effective tactics, projects and programs. Always test those tactics against the big picture.

We can also use Strategic Thinking Simplicity in our personal lives to find greater fulfillment and better relationships.

Use systems thinking as the foundation in your daily activities for better, more consistent results. Create a culture of systems thinking in your life and organization and reap the rewards of achieving all of your desired outcomes.

Simplicity Keys

➢ Always use systems thinking in planning, execution and day to day operations.
➢ Take the helicopter view of the organization.
➢ Ensure you have determined the right outputs/outcomes.
➢ Create measures based on your desired outputs/outcomes.
➢ Understand the relationships between outputs, feedback, inputs and throughputs.
➢ Remember your environment and what is changing.
➢ Use analytical thinking for building tactics
➢ Test the proposed tactics against the big picture

CHAPTER 4

Strategic Thinking Simplicity

*"Great leaders are almost always
great simplifiers, who can cut through
argument, debate, and doubt to offer a
solution everybody can understand."*
—General Colin Powell

You frequently hear people in organizations lament that we need to think more strategically. Where are the strategic thinkers when we need them?

In our day-to-day lives we are faced with many complex issues and challenges. We are trying to grow our organizations, meet tight deadlines, manage a crisis or just respond to the latest unreasonable request from a customer or supervisor. Where do you find the time to think strategically?

Fortunately, thinking strategically can be easily learned and applied to your daily life. Once you have mastered a few simple principles, you will find that strategic thinking can be used in both your business and personal life to dramatically improve your performance. It will also provide clarity of purpose which reduces stress and improves job satisfaction.

What is strategic thinking?

In simple terms, strategic thinking is the unwavering focus on the *desired outcomes* of your business, project or initiative or *"beginning with the end in mind"*. It can also be referred to as backward thinking, future thinking, long term thinking or high level thinking.

Strategic thinking is different from analytical thinking which is tactical, process oriented and linear. You will need both strategic and analytical thinking to be successful. The key is to start with strategic and then move to the tactical when you enter the execution phase. Great strategic leaders never lose sight of the desired outcomes even after they have moved into tactics.

We are not suggesting that strategic thinking is undisciplined or lacking of a process to follow. Actually, it is quite the opposite. By following a simple process, strategic thinking is possible for even the most analytical thinkers.

Strategic thinking is not the same as strategic planning. Many strategic plans are developed with very little strategic thinking. In those cases they should be more accurately called business plans. You need to do business or operational plans after you have developed your strategic plan. The absence of strategic thinking leads to a very high failure rate of any initiative and ultimately to your organization.

Strategic thinking is the critical piece of a successful strategic planning process. To successfully execute a strategic plan, you will need the continued strategic thinking focus *combined with* the sound tactics that come from analytical thinking.

Getting started

> *"Confusion is a great opportunity to simplify"*
> —Brian J. Rhiness

We like to start with encouraging people to take a "helicopter view" of the situation. This means getting above the daily obstacles that face the organization or individuals. Free yourself to think in broader terms of where you want to be, why you want to be there and what that looks like.

It is also a great idea to identify critical issues facing you or your organization at this early stage. By focusing on these critical points, we can ensure that throughout the thinking process we are developing solutions. If your strategic thinking does not lead to constructive results, you are wasting your time. Later in the model we will come back to the critical issues.

There is a very simple model that can support your strategic thinking process:

Strategic Thinking Simplicity model

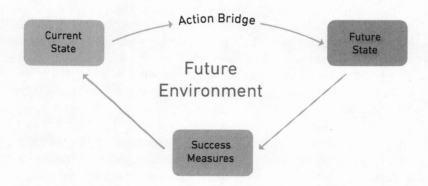

Thinking backwards means we start with the Future State. What is our vision for the future? Where do we want to end up? What are our desired outcomes? This requires a real, deep conversation. Forget the clichés and buzz words. You are looking for a clear, easily understood statement of your desired future state. A poor job at this stage will make the rest of the process a waste of time. Spend the time here to ensure real clarity. Leadership requires that clarity for communication and buy-in from stakeholders.

You are defining not only where you want to be, but why it is important and also who you are. A powerful vision, mission and core values will set a strong foundation for success.

This is also an important place to engage an effective project team. If team members can rally around an agreed upon outcome for the project they can improve buy-in, ensure accountability and improve the chances the initiative will succeed.

In your personal life, start with determining where you want to be. We know that this is the most powerful motivation for success. This may be setting career goals, defining the future with your partner or as simple as deciding where to go on vacation. Once you have a set destination, it is much easier to take steps to get there.

Scan the Environment

You will note in the middle of the model is Future Environment. This reminds us to do a complete and thorough future environmental scan prior setting our desired outcomes. Go back to your helicopter view for a clear picture of what is going on in your industry, jurisdiction or life.

Success Measures

How will you know if you are making progress? By putting success measures in place. These measures should be few in number and give you immediate feedback on how you are doing. The dashboard of your car is an excellent example of measures—at a glance it tells you everything you need to know about how your vehicle is doing and supplies immediate feedback on your actions. Do not wait for year end to measure your progress—that is too late.

Current State

Now is the time to make an honest and complete assessment of where you are today. This includes such things as resources, capacity, support and barriers to moving forward. A common approach is to use a SWOT (strengths, weaknesses, opportunities, threats) analysis. Use the helicopter again to get above day-to-day frustrations, institutional silos, egos and turf protection. These are all real obstacles to honest assessments.

We stress that this must be an honest assessment. If you gloss over real issues, you are not seriously thinking about success. Embrace skeptics in every phase of the planning process. They are your best friends.

Action Bridge

By this point in the model, we have a clear picture of where we want to be, a set of measures to test our progress in getting there and have an honest sense of where we are today. It is time to build the strategies, actions and tactics to bridge us from today to our desired future state.

Strategies are how we close the gap between where we are today and our desired future state. They are the ways, methods or group of activities we will use to get there.

Again, we stress the need for simplicity and clarity in the strategy statements. Avoid buzz words and general statements. We suggest starting the strategy statements with *"We will . . ."* If it is your personal life, make it an *"I will . . ."* statement. These are more powerful, action oriented statements and will be easier to understand and explain. Remember, someone will be responsible for getting this done. Will they have a clear understanding of what they need to do?

Under each strategy there must be a set of actions to achieve that strategy. **Actions** are the projects, initiatives or programs we will undertake to ensure the success of the strategy. We are still in strategic thinking mode. Get up in the helicopter again. What specific steps will get that strategy done? Once we have turned an action over to someone, they can come up with the specific tactics necessary to get results.

We have mentioned a number of times about keeping things simple and clear. This does not mean that the tasks needed to get the job done will not be difficult—most will be. If they are worth doing, odds are they will be difficult. Some may take many people years to accomplish and some will fail. You improve the odds of success by ensuring clarity of purpose and direction for those assigned the tasks. Then turn them loose, support them and trust them to get the job done.

Each project related to an action item can go through the same strategic thinking process. They can come up with their own desired outcomes, measures of success, current state assessment and then tactics.

Stress Test

You must stress test your strategies and actions against the critical issues discussed earlier. Ask this question: *"if we successfully implement these strategies and actions will they address the critical issues we identified?"* If you are not confident they will, keep going back and adding or adjusting the strategies and actions until you have the package you need to move forward.

Summary

There are countless planning models out there today. Some are good, many are far too complicated and others are just a waste of time. The bottom line is that all models including the one described in this chapter are flawed. Find one that works for you. It is not about the model, it is about the engagement of people and the conversation. Keep in simple. Building and implementing a successful strategic plan does not need to be difficult. By using strategic thinking and a simple planning model such as the Strategic Thinking Simplicity model, you will see a dramatic improvement in the results you achieve.

Simplicity Keys

> Start with your desired future state
> Scan the future environment
> Establish success measures to monitor progress towards your desired future state
> Do an honest assessment of your current state—identify crucial issues facing you and your organization
> Embrace skeptics
> Build your Action Bridge to take you from where you are today to your desired future state
> Measure your progress toward your future state
> Use "We will . . ." to get simple, clear strategy statements
> Test your strategies and actions against the critical issues facing the organization

CHAPTER 5

Strategic Management

"Strategy is about making choices, trade-offs;
it's about deliberately choosing to be different"
—Michael Porter

There are two organizations. The first has a clear strategic plan supported by everyone in their company and they have a reputation for superior execution.

The second group has a plan that was developed during an executive team golf retreat and it rests comfortably in the top drawer of the CEOs' desk. Staff may hear rumours of its existence and managers continually refer to the focus on execution.

Which organization will achieve better results?

The obvious answer is the first organization. If it is so obvious, why does the description for the second group fit what is really happening in most organizations today? Does it describe your organization today?

Research confirms that over 75% of strategic plans fail to deliver the desired results. The number one reason for failure is poor execution. An excellent plan poorly executed is a failure. A good plan well executed is a success.

Note that you *always* need a plan as the starting point. Execution without a plan is pure folly.

Our second organization has a focus on execution. If no one knows what the plan is, what is being executed? Pep talks from managers about digging in, working harder and other meaningless phrases only add to the confusion.

What is strategic management?

Strategic management is more than an annual planning retreat and a nice glossy document that no one looks at.

You need a simple, clear plan that outlines the desired outcomes for the organization going forward. The strategies and actions in the plan *must* be incorporated into business plans, operational plans, budgets and performance contracts throughout the organization. You must operationalize the plan. That is implementation.

Implementation is where we need full committed from everyone in the organization. There must be clarity around the strategies and actions, measures of success, timelines and accountabilities.

Execution takes time, focus and commitment. Strategies and actions needed to successfully implement your plan can take days, weeks, months or years. All of the above pieces must be integrated into the strategic management cycle.

Adopting the strategic management cycle will ensure that your organization progresses to your desired future state while building and sustaining high performance year after year.

Strategic Management Cycle model

Success in strategic management requires you to follow some simple but vital steps. The work, discussions and decisions within each step may be difficult but the steps are straight forward.

Support at the top

You need to start with a simple, clear strategic planning process. This means that **everyone** in the organization is aware of the steps, timelines and where they will be involved. We stress that everyone needs to be involved, at some stage, to ensure support throughout the organization. We use a **"Plan to Plan"** discussion with senior management prior to starting the planning process to map out the steps, engage the necessary stakeholders and establish timelines.

The process must be actively supported by senior management to ensure commitment throughout the organization. Setting the direction for the organization going forward is a primary responsibility of senior management and it cannot be delegated. The activities related to carrying out the planning process can be delegated to a small team or secretariat. This team can be established on a permanent basis to ensure that strategic management practices are fully integrated throughout the organization. The team must have direct accountability to and support from senior management. We strongly recommend the use of outside facilitation for the planning process. This brings a more balanced approach and eliminates concerns around bias, hidden agendas and favouritism. An outside facilitator can ask the tough questions that those in the organization may be reluctant to bring forward.

People support what they help create

You must involve all key stakeholders right from the beginning of the process. Who are your key stakeholders? A key stakeholder is anyone that can have an impact on the success or the failure of your plan. People support what they help to create. So get them involved from the start. You do not need everyone in the room at every step. But everyone should be clear on where, when and how they will have input into the process. Engaging stakeholders speeds up the strategic management process and dramatically improves your chances of success.

You will receive all kinds of input and some of it will be hard to accept. It is very important to *embrace skeptics.* These folks are your best friends. You need skeptics to test the validity of all parts of your plan. Don't confuse skeptics, who ask the tough questions and push for a better product, with cynics that just want to disrupt the process. Purge cynics from the process and your organization.

"Skeptics are your best friends"
Stephen Haines

Many organizations continue to see strategic planning as a secret process to be undertaken by a limited number of people at the top of the organization. They roll out a plan using the *"Decide—Announce—Defend"* (D.A.D.) model which ensures limited support and therefore limited success. In most cases it is a total failure.

Now the hard part

You now have a draft plan developed by a broad range of stakeholders. It clearly sets out the direction for your organization, and the strategies and actions necessary to make it happen. *Are you finished?* No, that was the easy part.

Now you must implement the plan. You are entering the execution phase where most organizations struggle. We strongly recommend a **Plan to Implement** discussion. This may be one meeting or a series of meetings depending on the size and complexity of your organization. Plan to Implement should take place a month or two after the planning retreat. This gives everyone time to digest all of the great stuff that came out of the planning retreat. This is another way of saying time for *"sober second thoughts"*.

Planning retreats are great and a vital step in strategic management. The discussion, ideas, team building and passion that come out of these sessions cannot be replaced. The question that must be answered in Plan to Implement discussions is: *can we actually implement all of this?* In my experience, no plan ever comes out of this step unscathed. That is OK. Some strategies will be given a higher priority. Some will be postponed until next year. Some may be dropped. All strategies must be matched against the ability of the staff in the organization to get them done. Always remember that you have on-going operations that cannot stop just because you have a new plan. If you are totally comfortable with your draft plan, you probably are not pushing hard enough. A good strategic plan should challenge the organization to higher places and be difficult to achieve. Anything worthwhile will be a challenge.

You must be prepared to make some difficult decisions.

> "The essence of strategy is
> choosing what not to do"
> —Michael Porter

All of the strategies and actions that you have agreed on must go into operational plans throughout the organization. This is where people will see their day to day efforts connected to the strategic plan. They must have sufficient funding to successfully complete their new assignments. Budget decisions are never easy, but you cannot move forward without them. What are you going to stop doing to reallocated funds? These are difficult decisions that must be made to ensure success of the strategic plan. Leadership failure frequently occurs at this stage.

New initiatives must be given full support or people will very quickly realize that the strategic plan is not worth the paper it is written on. Senior management must take on an advocate role to send clear messages of the importance of each initiative. The term "cheerleader" is often used but it is much more than "rah rah" and canned platitudes. It is daily support in communications, resources and rewarding those that reach milestones in strategic initiatives.

Who is accountable?

Another vital piece is ensuring that someone is accountable for each action or initiative. It must be an individual person—not a division, job title or committee. There must be a face for every action so people know who is taking the lead and is responsible. Most initiatives will require more than one person to get the job done but there is only one lead person. That person's performance contract must include this piece of work. If performance contracts, throughout the organization, do not change significantly with the approval of a new strategic plan it is impossible to execute. People will only do what they are being measured on.

The responsibility for the successful implementation of the plan starts with the senior executive team and should cascade clearly through the organization.

Strategic management cycle

On the cycle you can see that we have covered the planning phase and implementation steps. This is not the time to "drop the ball". We must continue to push to get actions completed, follow through on commitments and make all necessary changes. The plan must be reviewed on a regular basis and a transparent planning and updating process instituted. It is a cycle because the process we just covered will continue. Updates will lead to reviews of the vision, mission and values and monitoring of the measures. Every update has the potential for improvements to the plan. As we make those improvements our strategies and actions will change. Those changes will mean changes to budgets, operational plans and performance contracts. We will act on those follow through on commitments. Then we are into the next round of updates. Updates should be at least quarterly or more often if circumstances require it.

Stakeholder engagement and the future environmental scan are at the centre of the cycle. They should be top of mind at all times and not just when we do planning. Everyone in the organization should be constantly scanning for things that might affect the organization. We must be connecting with all key stakeholders regularly to ensure they support what we are doing. Their support means the difference between success and failure of everything we do.

When the strategic management cycle becomes "the way we do business" you will be well on your way to ensuring you achieve the superior results your organization is capable of. The management cycle is a living process that keeps going around pushing you toward your desired future state.

Simplicity Keys

> Never forget: execution without a plan is folly
> Implementation requires the full commitment from everyone in the organization
> Remember that execution takes time, focus and commitment
> Remember that people support what they help create
> Be prepared to make difficult decisions
> Stop doing some things to reallocate resources
> Ensure regular updates

SECTION 2

GETTING THE MOST OUT OF YOUR PLANNING PROCESS

CHAPTER 6

Getting the most out of your strategic planning process

*"You would not believe how difficult
it is to be simple and clear"*
—Jack Welch

Strategic planning is not fun. Anyone that has been involved in a planning process will probably agree with that statement. It is, however, one of the most important (we would argue *the most* important) roles of a leader to set and execute the strategic direction of the organization.

It is possible to carry out a very successful strategic planning process that is relatively painless and may even be enjoyable for most participants. There are a few things that you can do make a strategic planning process memorable for the right reasons.

Start with the people

Most groups when thinking about a planning process will start with the location, facilities and activities. *Start with the people*. Having the right people involved is the most important factor in any planning process. These are the people who know what is going on, have a vested interest in the future of the organization and will be tasked with implementing the plan. They need to be involved from day one. We will discuss more about the right people in the chapters on Plan to Plan (p. 38) and Stakeholder Engagement (p. 47).

A key person in the process is the outside facilitator. This person will make or break your planning process. We always encourage organizations to use an outside person to guide the process, even when the organization has a top notch planning group. An effective outsider brings a different tone to the process and will ensure that organizational issues and egos get left at the door. The planning process is about getting a good planning document and at the same time having people feel good about their involvement.

One caution when hiring outside help: Be wary of individuals or companies that tell you that the planning process will take months or even years to complete. If they give you that pitch—show them the door. We have seen far too many examples of consultants spending years "helping" organizations build the perfect strategic plan and leaving the organization frustrated and without any plan. There is no such thing as a perfect strategic plan.

Your hired help should be able to work with you to deliver a draft plan in a few weeks. As you will see by following the process in this book, a draft plan can be delivered very shortly after a simple two day planning retreat.

Will this plan be perfect? No.

Can you start implementing it immediately? Yes.

Which do you think is more important? A reality that must be accepted from the start is that any plan is flawed the moment it is written. The upside is that the plan is a living document and can easily be adjusted to meet things that change and it will improve as we continue to make those adjustments.

Another caution: hiring someone to write your plan for you. This is a total waste of money, no matter how big or famous the person or company may be. You will never implement a plan written by someone else. As the book will show, you can undertake a simple, cost effective process that has a much better chance of being successfully implemented. There are no short cuts.

Once you have the right hired help in place, they should help guide you through the steps to get an implementable plan in place. Here are the **must have** steps:

1. Plan to plan
2. Engage stakeholders
3. Get the most out of your planning retreat
4. Plan to implement
5. Schedule regular update sessions

These few simple steps will ensure that your planning process is both effective and enjoyable.

We will cover each of these steps in upcoming chapters.

Simplicity Keys

> ➤ Hire an outside facilitator to guide the process
> ➤ Start with getting all of the right people involved
> ➤ Do not hire someone to write your plan
> ➤ Follow the **must have** steps for getting the most out of your planning process

CHAPTER 7

Plan to Plan

Before you launch into a planning process you must *plan to plan*. This is a critical step in ensuring that the planning process is fruitful. There are many important steps in planning, this is the one step that will absolutely make or break your process. We have turned down contracts because organizations have felt this step is not necessary—they want to just get going. Their process will fail and we would not feel comfortable taking their money knowing that. In some cases organizations have come back to us after an expensive and painful lesson and we have started again with a plan to plan. Don't waste your time and money, do it right the first time.

It is strongly recommended to hire outside help in building and facilitating your planning process. It is that outside person that should be guiding you through these early stages.

There are a number of reasons that the Plan to Plan is critical. Firstly, you need the senior leadership in the organization on side. They must clearly demonstrate that this is their process and that they are fully committed to it. The plan to plan cannot be farmed out to anyone else in the organization. The CEO or group lead must be in the room and be part of setting all aspects of what will happen in the planning process. It has been mentioned previously, that the Simplicity planning process can be used at any level of any organization. In the plan to plan stage, we are looking to ensure the lead decision maker, for who the plan will apply, is driving the process. Follow the *Plan to Plan Checklist* for the questions to ask of the organization leadership. If the lead decision maker is not present, walk away.

Plan to Plan Checklist

o What are the desired outcomes from the planning process?
o What are the critical issues facing the organization?
o What is your organization . . . ?
   • Doing well?
   • Not doing well?

o What are successful organizations you know . . . ?
   • Doing well?
   • Doing that we can copy or improve on?

o What are the critical issues facing your clients/partners/industry?
o Prepare a detailed environmental scan prior to the planning retreat.
o Who are our key stakeholders?
o How and when will we involve key stakeholders?
o How and when will we report back to stakeholders?
o Are planning event details in place?
o When do we need a draft plan?
o When do we intent to implement the strategic plan?

At this point, please jump forward in the book and read the chapter on change (pg. 97). This will help you have a better understanding of why the Plan to Plan is critical to the strategic planning process. The time you spend here is the most valuable.

A successful planning process is about having the right conversation, so you need the right people involved. Much of the time in a plan to plan meeting is spent on *the right people*. Who are they? How do we involve them? When do we involve them? If you are going to err do it on the side of involving more people. This does not mean holding a huge event with a cast of thousands. Some people can be involved prior to an actual planning retreat. This can be done through staff input sessions, surveys or one on one discussions with key stakeholders. You are looking for as much input as possible as you move into the planning phase. The quantity and quality of input you receive prior to planning will determine the success of the entire planning and execution process.

In the plan to plan, we want to look at how we see the entire planning process rolling out. How long will each step take? Are there critical deadlines? When do we want a draft plan in place? When is the board expecting to approve a draft plan? When do we want to hold a plan to implement meeting?

We will want to get back to people. How will we report back to staff and other key stakeholders? Folks that have had a chance to supply input will be looking to see what you have come up with. Do not disappoint them. You should consider a second round of feedback from key stakeholders based on a draft plan. When the time comes to approve a draft strategic plan, one of the first questions asked is "how will stakeholders react to this?" You should have a gut feel when you answer that question and there is a simple way of determining it—*ask the stakeholder*s. These are the people that will make or break your strategic plan. You need their help. It is our experience that people are eager to help if the process is clear, open and honest.

An issue that we sometimes encounter is the feeling that the planning process is TOP SECRET, so therefore it must involve very few people and be strictly confidential. Get serious! That is nonsense. With a few minor exceptions, maybe hostile takeovers and military invasions, no planning process needs to be secret. If it is kept secret, the chances of it ever being successfully implemented are zero. If someone suggests the need for secrecy, look for another agenda. To date, we have not participated in a "secret" process and do not wish to. Usually after that initial suggestion and the plan to plan discussion a more open process is embraced.

A good plan to plan involves the right people in the right ways and begins the robust conversation that is the backbone of a successful strategic planning.

Simplicity Keys

➤ Hold a Plan to Plan with the key decision makers
➤ Follow the Plan to Plan checklist
➤ The outside facilitator should guide the Plan to Plan
➤ Focus on a robust conversation with all stakeholders

CHAPTER 8

The Planning Retreat

"Management is doing things right,
leadership is doing the right things"
—Peter F. Drucker

The planning retreat is the most high profile event in the strategic planning process. It normally generates the most attention, discussion and worry. If we are following the simple steps in the Simplicity planning process, this is just one more step. The work we have done leading up to the planning retreat will ensure that we get maximum value of the time that people are committing to it. *Do not organize a retreat until you have completed the Plan to Plan.*

This is your process. Work with your outside facilitator to ensure that it is meeting your expectations. Much of that work will have been done in the Plan to Plan.

We need to ensure that the right people are in the room. This discussion will be held in the Plan to Plan. The number of people is not as important as having the right people. The senior decision makers should know who needs to be in the room for the discussion to give them the desired results. As a bare minimum you will need the board members, executive team, managers and outside stakeholders that may add to the favour of the discussion. Adjust the participants to fit the organization or division conducting the planning process.

The principal purpose of the planning retreat is to have a great *conversation*. You must create an environment that will allow for that conversation to happen before, during and after the planning retreat. The discussion before will involve key stakeholders and can in the form of surveys, focus groups and team meetings. Your retreat should not be a secret. Let people know it is being held, encourage their input and promise to get back to them after the event with draft documents. This will keep the rumour mill quiet and help down the road when we want to implement the plan.

After the event get back to the key stakeholders as soon as possible with draft documents for their feedback. People are watching. The longer you wait the more suspicion will arise and trust will deteriorate. Even if you go back out with very preliminary thoughts from the retreat and stress that it is a work in progress, you will build good will with your stakeholders. It is recommended that some draft materials get back to key stakeholders within a week of the retreat. Waiting weeks or months before getting back is asking for trouble.

To ensure a great conversation at the retreat follow some basic good facilitation principals. It is a safe place for people to express their ideas and feelings. Leave your cell phones and other devices outside (have fun with financial penalties if someone's device goes off) and remove as many other distractions as possible. The facilitator is in charge. This means that all participants (even the CEO) are equal participants. Embrace skeptics and accept all ideas as having merit. This is no time for group think. It is the time to ask the tough questions about the future of the organization, where we are today and how we can best get to our desired future state.

Prepare and distribute as much background material as possible prior to the retreat. This should include a rigorous environmental scan and an in-depth current state assessment. If you are going to survey key stakeholders do so prior to the retreat. This is an opportunity to use the outside facilitator to handle the surveys. This provides the facilitator with a chance to get to know the stakeholders and the issues facing the organization. Share all background material and survey results with participants, prior to the retreat so they have a chance to prepare. A review of survey results at the start of the retreat sets the stage for an open discussion on the issues facing the organization.

The retreat should be held away from the organization headquarters. A comfortable meeting room with room for breakout sessions is advisable. Do not hold the planning retreat in conjunction with recreational activities. Golf is a great sport but does not mix with a planning retreat. If golf is on the agenda, it is the agenda. This is business and must be treated as such. Keep the attire causal.

The facilitator will set the tone for the event. It is important to stay on schedule and maintain the principles of respect and common curteousy for all participants. The use of technology should make sense for the event. Low tech options work well. Flipcharts are still the best option for recording participant thoughts. People like to see their ideas recorded and displayed. During the process, we will constantly come back to ideas generated, so keep them on the walls for all to see. Identify a staff person from the organization to work with the facilitator to record on the flipcharts and to be responsible for keeping all retreat materials. This same person should be responsible for working with the facilitator on the draft strategic plan.

A good facilitator will keep the process out of the face of participants and ensure all energies are spent on a rigorous conversation. Start the retreat with recording participant thoughts on desired outcomes for the planning process, critical issues facing the organization and a review of any survey results.

The planning retreat is a great opportunity for team building. There are many team building exercises that will work well and fit your organization. Whatever you choose ensure that it does not take up major chucks of time. This can be another topic for the Plan to Plan meeting agenda.

At the end of the planning retreat there must be enough work done to allow for the development of a draft strategic plan. This means that all parts of this section of the book will be complete at the end of the retreat. How long should the retreat take? With good pre-retreat work, a two day retreat is ideal. Longer retreats are recommended in some cases but there must be very good reasons to commit participants for the extra days. In large organizations longer retreats can be used to hold a planning session for the whole organization and then sessions for each individual division. By tying the planning sessions together you will keep everyone focussed on the shared vision and how each part can support achieving it.

A well run retreat can be enjoyable (or at least painless) and provide the organization and participants with a strong launching pad to move forward.

Simplicity Keys

> Prepare and distribute background materials prior to the retreat
> Make sure you have the right people in the room
> Let the outside facilitator guide the retreat with support from organization staff
> Remind everyone that the facilitator is in charge and that all participants are equal (even the CEO)
> Assure everyone that this is a safe place to express ideas and feelings—embrace skeptics
> Avoid group think
> Eliminate outside distractions - do not hold the retreat in conjunction with recreation activities
> Consider teambuilding activities
> A two day retreat is ideal

CHAPTER 9

Stakeholder Engagement

"No one person is as smart as all of us"
—Brian J. Rhiness

The term "key stakeholders" has been used frequently in our discussions so far. You will have noted that stakeholder engagement is at the very centre of the strategic management cycle model. The reason for this focus is that people are the single most important part of strategic planning. That statement may seem silly. Unfortunately, it is also so silly that many organizations and their leaders refuse to involve the right people in their strategic discussions. If you take only one point from this entire book that point should be: ***involve all of the people necessary to ensure the success of your strategic plan.***

Take a pause at this point and scan the chapter on change again. The discussion on change will help you appreciate why you need to be thinking very carefully about your stakeholders at this stage. The more quickly and safely you can get them through the change curve to acceptance and on to commitment and passion the better. Consideration of their needs at this stage will save you time and money later as well as improving your chances of successfully implementing your plan.

Ask this question: how can we help our stakeholders to accept and commit to our strategic plan as quickly and easily as possible?

Who are these people? A key stakeholder is anyone that can affect the success of your strategic plan. Inside the organization they include board members, managers and all staff. Outside the organization, they can include shareholders, suppliers, customers, clients and partners. All of these people have a personal interest in the success of your plan. You need to engage them on a personal level. Collectively all of these people have the ideas, passion and commitment to make any plan work. Get them involved.

When to involve them? Involve them as early and often as possible. You cannot fake engagement. If you are not really looking for their involvement do not attempt to engage them. People will sense your lack of sincerity and rightfully punish you. Your plan will fail.

How to involve them? The best way to engage stakeholders is to ask for and use their input. This can be done through surveys, focus groups, involvement in planning retreats or having senior managers talk to individual stakeholders. Remember to embrace skeptics. People inside and outside the organization will have insight that you will need to consider. Ask for their ideas, concerns and recommendations. Record them and promise to get back to them with your responses and draft documents. We need to be clear with all stakeholders that we are listening to many people and cannot guarantee that all recommendations will be accepted. We can guarantee that all will be heard, duly considered and our best judgements will be used in building the plan. When we have a draft document, we will get it back to our stakeholders for feedback.

Caution: Asking stakeholders for their input and then ignoring it and them is worse than not asking. Staff surveys and input is a special case. If you ignore them, trust is gone and it is hard to retrieve. Future surveys will be a waste of time.

Simplicity Keys

➢ Stakeholders are anyone that can affect the success of your strategic plan—be sure to involve all of them as early and often as possible
➢ Use surveys, focus groups, individual conversations or invitations to the planning retreat to get their input
➢ Help stakeholders to accept and commit to your strategic plan
➢ Get back to them as quickly as possible with draft documents
➢ Respect their time and input
➢ Embrace your skeptics
➢ Ignore input, especially from staff, at your peril

CHAPTER 10

Future Environmental Scanning

"You cannot predict the future,
but you can create it"
—Peter Drucker

Planning is about the future. Before you get busy planning, stop and take a look at that future. That is critical to effective strategic thinking and any planning process. You must put some thought into what the future might look like for you and your organization. We've placed environmental scanning at the center of the strategic management cycle for a very good reason. Miss this step and your planning process is a waste of time and money.

Strategic Thinking Simplicity model

Future Environmental Scanning is simply a look at the future world through the lens of topic areas that may affect your organization. The Future Environmental Scan is at the heart of the Strategic Thinking Simplicity model. We are looking at future trends, projections, opportunities and risks that may face you and your organization in the coming years. We do this *prior to starting the planning process* to ensure we have as much information as possible to make sound decisions.

As always, we recommend that you include as many stakeholders as possible in the scanning process. What are the critical issues facing each part of your organization? What are your suppliers, customers, clients and investors facing? What does the economy and political scene look like where you operate? The more questions you ask, the better the scan. Your internal people have the best focus on what is happening related to your industry, products and services—use them. In some cases you may need to go to outside experts for specialized intelligence.

Remember our helicopter view. Get above today's issues. Broaden the discussion and look at any and all possibilities. What seems crazy might just happen! If you only look at today, your planning will get stuck in today and it will be impossible to really move forward.

A thorough scan should cover areas including: your industry, stakeholders, political/regulatory, customers, competition, technology, financial, the natural environment, social, reputation, brands, demographics and any other issues specific to your organization.

For each of these topic areas we need to ask three key questions;

- What?
- So What?
- Now What?

For example:

- *What* is the trend?
- *So What* does that mean to our organization?
- *Now What* do we need to do to prepare for it?

Use the scanning process to build teams. Assign topic areas to groups of staff and have them come back with their thoughts to share with the entire organization. Embrace skeptics and people that push the boundaries of your thinking. Remember, no one can predict the future. We can however create it through unique ideas.

Be on the look-out for "black swans". A must read is <u>The Black Swan</u> by Nassim Nicholas Taleb. Effective future environmental scanning is looking for things that at one time were unimaginable but are now taken for granted. Identify those unexpected events that could affect your organization. What are the potential transformational technologies or business models and how would they affect you?

There are many examples of new business models, technologies or trends that changed the world for organizations. This can be either positive or negative depending on how your organization responds. Look at the music industry, computers, cell phones or social media for real life examples.

The results of your future environmental scan will provide a solid foundation for your strategic planning process. Use the Strategic Thinking Simplicity model to bring those great ideas to life.

Simplicity Keys

➢ Complete a rigorous Future Environmental Scan prior to planning retreat
➢ Involve key stakeholders in the scan—what is happening in their world?
➢ Take the helicopter view—do not get stuck in today issues
➢ Ask: *What? So What? Now What?*
➢ Use the Future Environmental Scanning process to build teams within the organization
➢ Look for "Black Swans"
➢ Embrace skeptics

CHAPTER 11

Future State

*"If you don't know where you are going,
any road will take you there"*
—George Harrison

You need a vacation. You get busy booking hotel rooms, airplane tickets and rental cars. Suddenly you realize that you have not yet decided where you are going on vacation. That is silly. Who would start taking actions without knowing where they are going?

The answer unfortunately is individuals and organizations every single day. People are directed to get busy, work harder and focus without a clue of where they are going. How does anyone know if they are helping or hurting? How do you measure progress, without a clear understanding of where you are going?

All of the build up and preparation so far in this book brings us to the most critical part of the strategic planning process. All pieces of the process are important and your plan will suffer if you do a lousy job of any part. Getting the right people in the room and doing a rigorous environmental scan provides the solid foundation for this critical conversation: your future state. If you mess up the discussion on your future state, your plan will absolutely fail. Do not under any condition, start the formal planning conversation at any other point on the Strategic Thinking Simplicity model. I will stress again; **the success of your strategic plan is tied to the future state discussion and decisions.**

Strategic Thinking Simplicity model

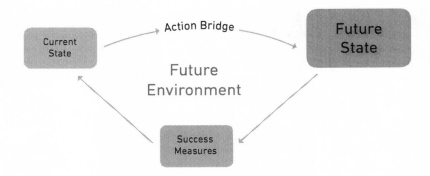

In the Strategic Thinking Simplicity model the future state is on the right side. This implies that it is our destination. It is where we want to end up. Some call it their desired outcomes. You can refer to it with any terminology that makes sense to you or your organization. In his book <u>The Seven Habits of Success People</u> Stephen R. Covey refers to this as "beginning with the end in mind". As you may recall from the earlier section of this book, beginning with the end in mind is the foundation of systems thinking.

Your future state has three parts:

- Vision
- Mission
- Core Values

Everything that is done in the strategic planning process follows what is done here. We will be building success measures, strategies and actions based on where we want to end up. A well thought out vision, mission and set of core values will make the steps that follow much easier and clear for everyone involved.

Vision

Start with setting your vision.

A vision is our view or image of what the ideal future looks like for us. It is our future hopes, dreams and aspirations, even if they are never totally attainable. The vision should be a positive and energizing statement of where we want to be at some point in the future. Successful people have used this basic approach forever.

Many people are skeptical of "the vision thing" and rightfully so. Many visions are meaningless drivel that could apply to any person or organization in the world. Make your vision specific to you. This is what success feels like, looks like and tastes like to you. We are talking about the future state so this is the vision of where you see yourself or the organization at some point in the future. Pick a point in time that is realistic. For organizations a good time is five years out.

An exercise that we like to use with groups is to ask each person to take a couple of minutes and write a newspaper headline for that day, five years in the future. They are playing editor for a day. The headline should say something about the organization. What do you want it to say? They are not writing the article, just the headline. That requires them to be clear and concise but get across what they aspire to be. It is amazing what comes out of this exercise.

Put the ideas up on flip chart and start playing with the words. Themes will emerge. As with the newspaper headline, the vision should be a nice crisp, clean statement.

Do not give up if the vision does not come easily. This statement is critical. Take a break if necessary and come back to it. During planning retreats, we will not let the group move on in the planning process until we have a working vision statement. Without it, further conversations are a waste of time. Remember our vacation example above—you must know where it is you want to go.

Mission

Once you have your vision you can set your mission. The mission is getting a little more specific. It must convey our unique purpose. Why do we exist? What business are we in? What do we produce or provide? Who do we serve? Those questions can be asked and answered for a person or an organization.

In many cases, this conversation is much easier for both individuals and organizations. If you are an established business you know the answers to the questions above. Test those assumptions. The world is changing very quickly and new business models and competitors are springing up daily. This is a great time for a conversation around those questions. Are you sure you are clear on who you serve and why? Are you producing the right things for the market today? The work you did in the environmental scan will be very helpful here. Open the floor to a real discussion on those key questions. A good facilitator should challenge your thinking and push for deep understanding of who you really are. A new mission may be exactly what you or your organization needs to relight the fires.

Check out the mission statements of other organizations. They can usually be found on their web sites. You can learn a lot about what works and what does not from the experience of others. When you see a mission statement, ask yourself if it is clear, if you can understand it and if it reflects the image the organization is trying to portray. Ask the same questions of your own mission statement.

Another test of your vision and mission statements is to ask if you would be proud to have them on your business card and web site. Also, could you explain them quickly to anyone who asked?

Core Values

The final piece of the future state is the core values. Core values are how we act, or should act, while fulfilling our mission and achieving our vision. It is the way we do business. They guide our daily behaviours and will define us as an individual or organization. It is the core values that really set the culture of any organization.

Setting core values is not just listing a bunch of words that everyone feels should be there. Most organizations will use standard words such as: respect, integrity, trust, accountability etc . . . These are great words and should be part of every organization and the principles by which we operate as individuals. What takes them from meaningless words to foundations of our culture is to *define them*. Defining them does not mean opening the dictionary. It means having a conversation around the words and having your unique definition attached to the word in all documents. Then you have *to **live the core values***. This means everyone in the organization, every single day. People will see very quickly if core values are real or meaningless words.

The word accountability is a favorite. We will see in upcoming chapters that accountability means having a name and a timeline attached to an action and the expectation that the person will get the job done. If the job does not get done, that person is held to account and there are consequences. If an organization is known for finger pointing, excuses and the blame game, using the word accountability is a joke and no one is laughing. Everyone in the organization, starting at the very top must support and live by the same core values. You are being watched.

People at the top of the organization are being watched more closely than anyone else. If one of your core values is integrity but the CEO has a different definition for himself/herself than for others, you do not have integrity. If senior executives treat their reports badly do not expect a culture of respect. More so than ever, especially with cell phones and YouTube, you are being watched as an individual and as an organization 24/7.

There is the story of the board of directors of Enron temporarily suspending their core values on occasion, so that they could do certain things. We all know what those things were. You cannot suspend core values. You either live them or you do not.

The violation of core values is frequently where organizations and individuals get into trouble. The damage to your reputation can take a long time to repair.

Defining your core values will allow you to test them in specific circumstances. They should be part of every training program for new staff. Over time, how you live and demonstrate those core values to your customers, partners and staff will create the stories that become the culture of great organizations.

Simplicity Keys

> Start your planning discussion with your Future State, incorporating your vision, mission, and core values
> Make the vision statement meaningful and specific to you, incorporating your desired outcomes
> Do not move on in planning until you have a working vision statement
> Ask yourself: would you be proud to have your vision and mission statements on your business card?
> Define and live your core values

CHAPTER 12

Do Measures Matter?

"The manager asks how and when;
the leader asks what and why"
— Warren Bennis

The 2013 annual letter from Bill Gates is a powerful document. It is a must read for anyone trying to get results in their business or personal life. Go the Bill and Melinda Gates Foundation web site and print it off. Keep it for future reference. In a few pages Mr. Gates outlines the need for the right measures matched with the outcomes you are trying to achieve and the power of constant feedback. The example used of the vaccination work done by UNICEF is more inspiring than any business case study you will ever read.

Measures do matter.

We all know the old saying—*what gets measured gets done*. It is absolutely true. Sadly, measuring our progress is not something that is done well or in many cases done at all. Measurement brings clarity of performance and accountability. Those two words strike fear into many people. As Bill Gates points out, it also brings clarity of purpose and progress. Those words should be a call to action not just for the good work done by global charitable groups but for any organization trying to be successful.

Feedback is one of the cornerstones of systems thinking. We start by setting the outcomes we wish to achieve and build measures to assess how we are doing in moving toward those desired outcomes. Without accurate measures we have no clue if we are moving in the right direction.

Strategic Thinking Simplicity model

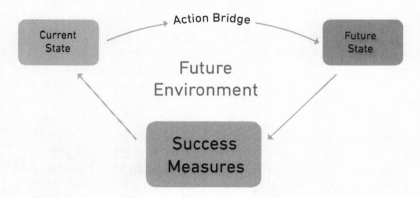

What are Measures?

Measures are simply assessments of progress to ensure continual improvement towards the desired future that has been set. They answer the questions:

- ❖ How will we know if we are being successful?
- ❖ How will we know if we are getting off track?
- ❖ What corrective actions are needed to get back on track?

Measures are the way we keep score. Try playing or watching any sport without keeping score. Not only is it boring, it is impossible to motivate the players or fans. If there is no focus, no one can make adjustments in their game plan. Do we need more offense or defense? Imagine a famous coach giving an inspiring speech between periods without knowing the score. That would be ridiculous, and it is happening in organizations every day. How are managers motivating staff with no scorecard?

How to Measure

First, keep it simple. You do not need to measure thousands of things. Envision the dashboard of a car. There are a few key things that will give a quick assessment of how things are going. With a quick glance you can see how fast you are going, how much gas you have left and kilometers driven. Warning lights also come on if you are low on oil, there is a problem with your tires or you need to have the engine checked. These simple measures take the guesswork out of driving a car. Take those same principles and apply them to planning in your business or personal life.

Measuring the progress on your strategic plan is not the same as collecting and analyzing all of the data needed to operate your organization on a daily basis. That data is vital. Some of it may be helpful in assessing your progress as an organization but it can also bury everyone in mounds of data with no conclusion. The dashboard approach gives you some valuable quick indicators that will tell you how you are doing. Further analysis may be required to get to the root of any problems.

You will recall from our *Strategic Thinking Simplicity* model that we start by establishing our desired outcomes in our future state. The next step is to determine how we will measure progress toward that future state. What indicators will tell us if we are on track? The target will determine what and how you will measure. For example, if you have decided that you will finish a marathon next summer, measures would be keeping track of your daily and weekly training runs. If after one month you cannot walk around the block, some adjustments need to be made.

If your outcome is to be the leading provider of some high tech equipment to hospitals, then sales of that equipment is an obvious measure. Will waiting to the end of the year tell you if you have been successful? Yes and no. Year end sales or profits are *lagging indicators* and are of course important but are too late to make necessary adjustments. Lagging indicators are historical, quantifiable results, at the end of a period. You also need *leading indicators* such as daily, weekly and monthly sales. Leading indicators are predictive processes, activities and behaviours. Not all measures will be numbers. Feedback from your sales force and clients will tell you very quickly how you are doing. Getting out of the office and talking to staff and customers is a very good way of getting immediate feedback.

In training for your marathon, the lagging indicator is actually finishing the race. The leading indicators are those daily, weekly and monthly training runs that get progressively longer and easier.

In order for measures to be effective they must be meaningful to those that are looking at them. Take the time to assess or ask your stakeholders what they need to see and when. The board of directors will have some very specific needs, as will senior management, staff, shareholders, suppliers and customers. Feedback from all of these sources will allow you to make immediate adjustments or course corrections as you move toward your desired outcomes.

Look for a broad range of measures that cover things like quality, quantity, time and cost. Match those areas up with customers, employees, society, operations, stakeholders and, of course financials, and you have the foundation of an effective measurement system.

Measures should also be in place for your strategies and actions. This is the "how to" part of getting to our desired outcomes. By measuring all of the strategies and actions, we ensure that each of the individual pieces we have put in place on our *Action Bridge* are contributing to getting us from our current state to our desired future state.

Ensure that your measures are visible to those that need to see them. Secret measures do no good. Visible measures can motivate and keep everyone focussed on the right outcomes. If we know what we are measuring and who is responsible, we have true accountability. The right metrics drive the right behaviours.

Measures give us the milestones we need to celebrate successes, the data we need to adjust course quickly and the justification to stop doing some things.

Use measures as part of your strategic planning process to change your organization, your life or maybe even the world.

Simplicity Keys

➢ Remember: what gets measured gets done
➢ Set up your dashboard indicators
➢ Use leading and lagging indicators
➢ Remember that not all measures are numbers
➢ Ask stakeholders what indicators they need
➢ Link measures to strategies and actions as well
➢ Make measures visible
➢ Celebrate milestones

CHAPTER 13

Understanding Your Current State

Could you honestly and accurately assess how your organization is doing today?

We are not referring to your candid thoughts in the bar after work. We are talking about in front of your colleagues in an open, honest, realistic and comprehensive review of what is working and not working in your part of the organization. Most people will quickly say of course I could. In fact, most people find it difficult and even impossible.

In the strategic planning process, the current state assessment is where people will feel the most vulnerable. You are now talking about current performance. Egos, budgets, personal empires and respect of your colleagues are suddenly on the table.

Strategic Thinking Simplicity model

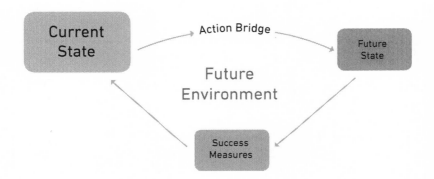

Up until this stage in the *Strategic Thinking Simplicity* model, we have been talking about environmental scans, desired outcomes and success measures. These are usually safe discussion areas for participants. We need to provide that same safe discussion space if we are to get a true assessment of where we are today. This is another vital piece in the strategic planning process. We have already established *where we want to be* with our future state (vision, mission, values) and we must compare that to *where we are today*. The gap between where we are today and where we want to be will be covered with the Action Bridge.

The current state assessment is a snapshot of where the organization is today. No judgements. We are looking for a realistic, comprehensive and honest discussion. Take our helicopter view again for that big picture perspective and then come back to earth for some of the very specific pieces. Remember to embrace skeptics; they are your best friends. This is not the time for general statements about how great we are or glossing over issues. As we move from our current state to our desired future state we know that things like existing structures, culture, egos, budgets and processes will be the biggest barriers to the changes we need to make. Put those issues on the table. In the upcoming chapter on change, we will cover the challenges facing you as you move to implementing your strategic plan. Check out the Iceberg and Change Curve (p. 98). Discuss them openly during your current state conversation. It is also important to be open about the financial state of the organization. As we work toward developing the strategies and actions that will be our Action Bridge, we need the most information possible in order to make the best decisions.

There are many different approaches to collecting the necessary information for a rigorous current state assessment discussion. Find one or a combination of approaches that works for you. We recommend the standard **SWOT** analysis.

SWOT stands for Strengths, Weaknesses, Opportunities and Threats. The strengths and weaknesses are internal to your organization. The strengths are those things that we can build on going forward. As always, we need to be specific and do not fall back on general statements and buzz words. The weaknesses are things that we will need to eliminate or cope with going forward. By identifying where we are vulnerable we can take steps through our strategies and actions to turn some of those weaknesses into strengths.

The Opportunities and Threats are external to the organization. What is happening in our industry, country or global marketplace that could impact us both positively and negatively? Some of this information will have been collected during the environmental scanning exercise earlier in your planning process. It is important to remember to take the discussion deeper than just making a long list of items. What are the real opportunities and how do we capture them? How can we turn potential threats into new opportunities? Opportunities are things we can exploit for our benefit and Threats are things we need to ease, eliminate or turn on their heads.

The SWOT process and the environmental scanning exercise are great opportunities to involve people throughout the organization and even outside partners and stakeholders. We want to gather as much useful information as possible as well as engaging as many people as possible. These are two places in the planning process where that works well. The better the information the better the decisions and the more people feel engaged the greater the chance that our strategies and actions will be successfully implemented.

You can create teams to work on various parts of the SWOT or have breakout sessions at staff meetings to gather input. Specific ideas on potential opportunities or identified weaknesses can be assigned to task teams to develop possible strategies and actions. The better quality of the work here, the better the strategies and actions will be at the next stage.

Reporting on the current state and the SWOT analysis is a great place for the CEO or group leader to demonstrate their support and commitment to the planning process. A summary of the key points and areas of concern and opportunity will show all people involved that they are being heard and that their efforts are important to the planning process. These are the same people you will be counting on to implement the strategies and actions to move the organization forward.

SWOT and environmental scanning are two exercises that should be more than an event completed yearly. There is a real advantage to these activities being on-going. Establish teams to monitor key areas and report back on a regular basis. The world around you is changing quickly. You cannot wait for an annual planning review to respond to a new threat or to grasp a new opportunity.

Simplicity Keys

- ➤ Have a realistic, comprehensive and honest discussion
- ➤ Take the helicopter view again
- ➤ Get specific
- ➤ Remember egos, budgets, structures, culture and empires are all in play
- ➤ Embrace skeptics
- ➤ Use SWOT
- ➤ Involve stakeholders again
- ➤ Have the CEO or group lead deliver the reporting
- ➤ Do not limit SWOT and Environmental Scanning to yearly events
- ➤ Establish teams to monitor key areas and report back regularly

CHAPTER 14

Build Your Action Bridge

Most people want to jump straight to actions. Forget the planning part and let's just get busy!

Busy doing what?

People need to know where they are today and where the organization is going. What is our destination? People want to contribute positively, and will, if given the right tools. Without a clear sense of what the desired outcomes are they will do something and it may or may not be what is needed.

Strategic Thinking Simplicity model

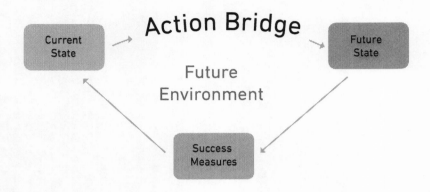

Following the *Strategic Thinking Simplicity* model, has taken us from the starting point of setting our desired future state, through establishing the measures of success and assessing our current state. Those steps were completed after doing a rigorous environmental scan. All of those steps, in that order, are absolutely essential if you are to be successful. Now we are ready to fill the gap between where we want to be and where we are today. We are going to build an Action Bridge to the future.

The Bridge

The Action Bridge is very simply the set of strategies and actions that we believe will take us from our current state to the desired future state that we have envisioned. If we have done a good job in the previous steps of the process, this part will be relatively easy.

The strategies are the how tos' of the process. They are the means to the end that we have set. We will build a group of activities, methods or specific ways that we will use to bridge the gap. It is important to be very specific in the language you use. The strategies you set will communicate to all those involved what your intentions are. Vague language means poor communication. We recommend using phrasing such as: *We will . . .*

For example: *We will expand operations into China*.

You are probably thinking that statement does not tell us how. Stay tuned.

The strategy is linked to our desired outcomes. If our desired outcome is to be a global player in our industry, then expansion into China fits. It clearly communicates our strategic intent.

Keep the number of strategies small to focus the organization. We recommend that no more than seven strategies be undertaken at any given time. Remember that the organization will have on-going operations and priorities. Overwhelming people with stuff that clearly cannot get done with existing resources is demoralizing and ensures that nothing will be successfully implemented.

The strategies should be a mix of external and internal. If we need to expand into China, there will be some internal things that we need to do. There may be some structural, management and governance changes that are needed. A good mix of strategies shows that you have thought through all of the pieces needed for success.

Time for Action

Under each strategy will be a list of actions. Those actions will turn the strategy into reality. The actions are the specific projects, initiatives, programs that we will undertake to ensure the success of the strategy. We must be very specific because someone is going to be assigned the task of getting this done. It will be in their work plan, so we need to be clear. Within each of the action items is where we deploy the tactics to support the action. From our example on China we will have very specific things that we will have to do to expand operations into China. Your people will know the answers, trust them.

While we assign one person to be the lead on any action, in fact the work will flow to teams throughout the organization. Clarity is essential as actions move through divisions, local branches and to personal performance contracts. It is now very personal, so a relentless focus on clarity of purpose is required. Each person should be able to link their performance contract to the actions they are working on, the strategy it supports and the desired outcome that will be achieved. Even on-going operations can be linked to demonstrate support for our desired future state.

There may be many actions to support a strategy. Each of those should have a project plan, timelines and measures of success. All of this should be in performance contracts for the individuals involved.

Updating your Strategies

We are often asked, how often should strategies be updated? The answer is whenever it makes sense to update them. That may be weekly, monthly or quarterly. Do not wait for annual updates. Your strategic plan is a living document. It should be the focus of the board and management. At every meeting there should be a review of the strategies and actions.

By updating the document and communicating it regularly, people can see progress. Individuals can be recognized for completion of projects. Remember to celebrate those successes. Each step is getting us closer to the fulfilment of the strategy and ultimately our desired future state.

Timing the updates of the strategies and actions will become obvious as you move along. If all actions have been successfully completed then a strategy may be done—major celebration! That strategy can be checked off or adjusted to set the bar higher.

All strategies and actions should be in one easy to find place. We recommend the Action Summary document. This document includes your vision, mission and core values so that they are always the focus. Each strategy is stated along with the list of all actions to support that strategy. Each action will identify the individual person assigned to lead it, the timeline and a place for status update.

Your strategic plan and the action summary are living documents. They should be updated regularly and communicated to all stakeholders. This is an opportunity for continuous communication of your priorities and your progress to the desired outcomes. Use the documents to ensure strategic focus on what is important. By continually updating you are also demonstrating the operational flexibility that is required for successful strategic execution.

You will not get every strategy and action right the first time. Being willing to maintain strategic focus on the outcomes you want and the necessary operational flexibility to adjust quickly as needed you dramatically improve your execution success.

Simplicity Keys

> Build your Action Bridge to cover the gap between where you are today (current state) and where you want to be (future state)
> Limit the number of strategies to a manageable number (no more than seven)
> Use clear language like "We will . . ." statements
> Don't micromanage - trust your people to supply the actions and tactics to support the strategy
> Record your strategies and actions in an Action Summary document to ensure continual focus
> Use the strategic plan and Action Summary as communication tools for stakeholders.
> Use regular plan updates to demonstrate strategic focus and operational flexibility
> Celebrate completion of actions and strategies

CHAPTER 15

Your Strategic Life Plan

The process we have used to build an effective strategic plan for an organization can also be used to create a strategic plan for your life. The *Strategic Thinking Simplicity* model is your guide to create a plan for your career, relationship, or lifestyle changes.

Strategic Thinking Simplicity model

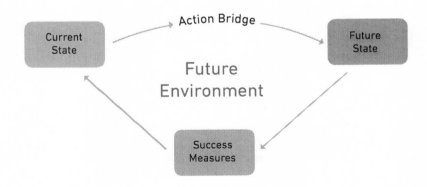

Scan Your Personal Environment

Start by doing an environmental scan, but in this case you are the centre of the universe. What do things look like in your world in the coming five years? What are your career prospects? How stable are your existing relationships? How will your health be going forward? Will changes in the economy affect you? Look for those "black swan" events. Things that do not seem realistic today but could happen. How would such dramatic events affect you? Spend some real time on these and other questions that are important to you in your life. Be honest with yourself and test your assumptions. Be sure to take notes. You will want to test the strategies and actions you develop against your environmental scan assumptions.

Define Your Future State

What is the vision of your ideal future? Your vision is your view of what your ideal future looks like. It will represent your future hopes, dreams and aspirations even if they are never fully attainable. Your vision statement should be an energizing, positive and inspiring statement. This is very personal to you.

If you use the front page of the newspaper exercise that we used in the Future State section, what would a front page headline in the newspaper five years from today say about you? You can develop a number of these to reflect your career aspirations, better relationships or changes you want to make in your health or lifestyle.

Picture this headline: ***Brian Rhiness wins the Iron Man Triathlon***

That is never going to happen!

It does give you the idea of a simple, clear vision of a future event around which to build a plan to achieve it. High achievers, be they Olympic athletes, successful business people, sports figures, musicians, artists, researchers, politicians or in any other walk of life have set lofty goals for themselves. By setting that seemly unachievable target you must set strategies and actions to push yourself out of your comfort zone. A good strategic life plan should do that.

Measure Progress

The next step in the *Strategic Thinking Simplicity* model is Success Measures. This is where we set how we are going to measure our progress toward winning the triathlon. Remember to keep the measures simple and easy to understand. In this case, things like times for swimming, running and biking are obvious. Benchmark today and keep a log of times to measure progress. If you do not know how to swim, there are some more basic measures like taking swimming lessons or getting a swim coach. You will recall that measures do not have to be numbers. They can be simple indicators of progress toward your desired future state. In our example, learning to swim is a very clear indicator of progress. Without that step, there is no chance of winning the triathlon.

Assess Your Current State

Time for a reality check. We need to assess where we are today. In our example, we will need to look at our current health situation and maybe get a doctor's opinion. Will our family and work life allow us the time to commit to training? Do we have the finances to commit? Do we have a bike, running shoes, swim suits and other resources needed to train? Will our partner and friends be supportive?

The same questions around structures, resources and culture that an organization must assess, you must assess for your personal life goals.

Action Bridge

Now is the time to build the strategies and actions that will bridge us from where we are today to our where we want to be in the future.

In the strategies and actions we must get very specific. If you do not know how to swim an obvious strategy is: *"I will learn to swim"*. Note that our terminology has changed from organizational strategies where it was *"We will . . ."* This is personal, it is about you. You are making this commitment so make it personal to you.

Actions under this strategy are the specific steps we will take to achieve the strategy. What will you need to do to learn to swim? Actions could be: sign up for swimming lessons, hire a swimming coach, get to the pool four times a week or even buy a swim suit. Each of those actions will help us on the path to our ultimate outcome—winning the triathlon.

You will need a number of other strategies related to running, biking, diet, financial support, adjusting work schedules and anything else needed to get you from your current state to your desired future state.

As you achieve various actions and even strategies, celebrate your success and create new ones. When you have learned to swim, that strategy is completed and deserving of a big celebration. A new strategy could be: *"I will swim 2 miles nonstop in open water"*. Since this is what you will need to do to complete an Iron Man Triathlon, you are staying focussed on your future state and adjusting your strategies accordingly. Actions now could be: start doing equivalent lengths of an indoor pool, start with short lengths in open water and join an open water swimming group.

You can set a number of visions for different parts of your life and use the same process to set the corresponding strategies and actions.

This is also a great process for couples. By setting down and having a shared vision it can bring you closer together. By building plans to achieve that vision together you will reduce misunderstandings and maybe even increase your happiness level—a future state bonus.

Simplicity Keys

➢ Set your desired future state or outcomes
➢ Make your own headline
➢ Involve your life stakeholders in the process
➢ Do an honest assessment of your current state
➢ Scan your environment
➢ Set up measures to monitor progress
➢ Build your Action Bridge to your desired outcomes
➢ Celebrate successes

SECTION 3

EXECUTION

CHAPTER 16

Successful Plan Execution

"Management is efficiency in climbing the ladder
of success, leadership determines whether
the ladder is leaning against the right wall"
—Stephen R. Covey

You have a plan.

That was the easy part. We know that 75% of strategic plans fail. All of those failed plans had brilliant words on paper. Virtually all of the plans failed at the execution stage. The organization failed to take the necessary steps to implement the great ideas they came up with.

In this section we will cover the obstacles you will face as you turn those great ideas in actions that get you the results you are looking for. We will also show you proven techniques to get past those obstacles and improve your chances of success.

You will note that we use the words execution and implementation interchangeably. Use the words in the way they are most meaningful to your organization.

The strategic plan is implemented through operational plans, annual plans, tactical plans, performance contracts, rewards and budgets.

The key pieces for successful strategic plan implementation are:

- ✓ Simple, clear strategies and actions
- ✓ Individual accountabilities for delivery of each action
- ✓ Clear, realistic timelines for delivery
- ✓ Regular check-ins on the status of each action project

To bring those key pieces to life we need: **Plan, People, Focus, Accountability and Resources**. If any one of these pieces is missing, your plan will fail. This section will pull all of these pieces together.

Throughout the book we have stressed the need for full commitment from the organization leadership. It is easy to give that commitment during the planning stage. When it comes to implementing the plan that commitment will be tested and many managers will go into hiding. A new plan will mean change. Change is hard. Everyone supports change until it affects them. As a manager, you have budgets, staff, programs and egos tied up in your part of the operation. The commitment to implement must start at the top and be supported throughout the organization, without exception. The slightest backtracking by anyone will send the signal that this process is not serious and we can wait it out. Be prepared to be relentless on execution.

You must have a plan that you are confident in. It will never be perfect and in most cases a good plan is good enough to get started. The plan is a living document which can and will be adjusted as you move forward. The execution process will bring all of the plan's flaws to light. What looks great on paper will get a reality check when someone is given the task of implementing a piece of it. If a strategy or action is wrong, admit it quickly and fix it immediately. This is not the time to dig in on something that everyone knows is wrong. People will need support and the flexibility to deliver their individual initiatives.

If you realize that the plan is really bad, admit it and start over. You cannot fake it. By starting over we are not suggesting taking months to redo it. The basics you did in your planning process are probably still valid. Take **one day** and bring the group back together. Start with what is great about the plan, then what is good and then what simply will not work. Commit to get going on the great and good stuff and fix the pieces you are not confident in. In most cases, you will find that some minor tinkering will give you the confidence in the plan to get going on execution.

This is the most important section in the book. The sections on Plan to Implement, Change, Action Summary, regular updates and getting back on track are the keys to your success. Read and then read them again. Keep the book handy and come back to this section every month for a refresher. For how long? You will know that answer when you get there. In most organizations and even for your life plan you will need at least one year of constant reinforcement before your strategic management cycle is working well. Until then you are in constant danger of going off the track.

Now let's getting executing.

Simplicity Keys

> Remember most plans fail at execution
> Bring your plan to life with: plan, people, focus, accountability and resources
> Remember that "good" is "good enough to get started"—the plan will never be perfect
> If something is wrong admit it quickly and fix it immediately
> Allow time for implementation—support, follow-up and constant reinforcement are critical

CHAPTER 17

Plan to Implement

It is vital to turn that strategic plan document into reality. If we do not take action on it, it will be a very nice document sitting on a shelf somewhere.

For most people execution is where the excitement is. Many will want to jump to execution without a plan. That is foolhardy and guarantees failure. Build a good plan first and then focus on great execution. This is where you put your battle plan in place and the tactics that will ensure your success.

We strongly recommend a Plan to Implement discussion prior to beginning execution. It is best to leave a little time between the planning retreat and the plan to implement session. By a little time, we mean a month or so. This gives time for participants to reflect on the discussion and ideas. It also gives time for reconnecting with your staff and other stakeholders to get their feedback on the draft plan.

This is another opportunity to get the right people in the room and ensure commitment to the execution process. Remember this is where plans fail, so get it right from the start.

You will recall from the previous chapter that we need: **Plan, People, Accountability, Focus and Resources.** In the Plan to Implement discussion we will start to build the foundation for those key pieces.

The Plan

Does your plan make sense?

This is code for sober second thoughts. Planning retreats are great for generating excitement and ideas. The space between that crazy new idea and something that can actually be implemented may be a bridge too far. Now is the time to say so. In practice, we have never had a draft plan coming from a planning retreat that has survived the plan to implement process intact. That is a very good thing. It means we are seriously looking at it and trying to get our heads around implementation. If we are just going to rubber stamp the draft document, it will never be implemented.

We need to look at what is missing. In many cases, organizations will forget their on-going operations in their desire to look to future. Do you have strategies in place to cover today as you move to tomorrow? What feedback did we get from stakeholders? Did some of our ideas with more thought generate even better ideas? Have we clearly stated what we expect done in the strategies and actions? Everything is open for challenge and discussion.

The strategies and actions must be very clear statements. We will be assigning these tasks to an individual. Will that person understand what we want done?

Take a hard look at your vision, mission and core values. Do those poetic words you created still resonate? Did we get some feedback that would make them better?

The Plan to Implement is also the time to get reports from teams that have been working on success measures, scenario planning or other special assignments coming out of the planning retreat. This extra work will greatly enhance the quality of the plan and give the execution process a boost.

People

The plan will not be implemented without people. That may sound blindingly obvious but most organizations do not involve the right people in the planning and implementation discussions. We encourage organizations to err on the side of involving too many people. That does not mean you need a cast of thousands at your planning retreat or in the Plan to Implement session. There are numerous techniques that can engage people in your process. Use focus groups before and after events to get input and feedback. Find processes that work for your organization and that people trust. The little bit of extra time spent engaging people at the start and throughout the process will pay off when you ask them to implement the new strategies and actions. The time to build support is at the start and at every step.

This will also be the first of many discussions on barriers to implementation. Do not skip over this piece by assuming that since you have a great plan everyone will jump on board. That will never happen. Be open about the barriers you face in executing your plan. Those barriers will include budgets, culture, existing structures, existing work plans, stakeholder concerns and lots of egos. Identify those barriers and start developing specific tactics to address them. We use the word "tactics" deliberately in this case because the approaches must be very specific and action oriented. We will discuss barriers to execution further in the chapter on change.

Accountability

Without assigning people to implement the action items you have decided on, it is impossible to achieve successful execution. By assigning people we mean individual people, not positions, committees or teams. There may be a team of people working on a project but we need to know who the lead person is that is being held accountable for getting that task done. Accountability is scary. In many organizations, keeping your head down and avoiding accountability is part of the culture. If that is the case in your organization, it must be changed. Accountability like most things starts at the top of the organization. The board must hold the CEO accountable for the successful execution of the strategic plan. The CEO will hold direct reports accountable for various parts of the plan and so on through the organization.

Accountability brings with it the expectation of support from those that are holding you accountable. At each level that support must be real. It starts with the clear strategy and action statements and a shared understanding between the person being held accountable and their supervisor of what success looks like. Build these new responsibilities into that person's performance contract. If their performance is measured on the strategic plan tasks they have a much better chance of being completed. It means ensuring people have the resources, time and feedback they need to succeed. People will determine very quickly if they are really being supported in what they are being held accountable for. If it is not real, they will run for the exits and the plan will fall apart.

In organizations with effective accountability systems, there is a culture of people actively seeking opportunities to lead actions items. They know that this is where promotions and future opportunities come from. Successful completion of assignments is cause for celebration and everyone enjoys being recognized for their achievements. Make these celebrations a regular part of board and management events.

Remember to tie rewards to the outcomes you want. If people are being rewarded for achieving the strategic action items in their performance contracts they have a much stronger motivation to get them done. If you do not adjust their performance contract, they will continue to do what they have always done because that is what they get rewarded for. There is the old saying "what gets measured gets done" which is true. A much more true statement is "what gets rewarded gets done".

Focus

It is easy to get distracted. Day to day commitments, the latest crisis and your supervisor's ever changing priorities will consume your time and take you off the strategic action items that you are committed to. To be honest, you may not really want to do them anyway so the latest crisis is a welcome relief. This is the reality of implementing a strategic plan. To get things done requires everyone to be obsessed about each and every item being successfully completed on time.

The focus must start with the leadership of the organization. We strongly recommend that every board meeting and senior management meeting begin with a review of the strategic priorities and update on progress. This regular review should be cascaded through the organization so that everyone is aware that the plan is important and we will execute the plan. The regular review can be completed very quickly and effectively by using the Action Summary Update. We will discuss it in an upcoming chapter.

It can also be useful to bring in an outside facilitator for the regular updates. The person that helped you build the plan is an obvious choice. An outside person can push the group and ensure that you are not skimming over things that are not being completed. After each review session the plan should look different. Things are getting done and new actions being added. The review is an active engagement and building event. The review is an ideal time to identify and celebrate the individuals that have successfully completed assignments.

Resources

The final piece of the implementation puzzle is resources. Without the necessary resources to accomplish the assigned strategic plan tasks, the person responsible is set up for failure. Nothing will destroy a leader's credibility quicker than making a big deal of a new strategic direction or initiative and not giving it the resources to achieve success. Everyone will know immediately if the initiative is real or just another management smoke screen. Life will be sucked out of the people involved and in most cases it will not really be launched.

By resources we mean: real dollars; people really assigned to the tasks and not off the corner of their desk; and open, public support from the organization leadership. This will require some adjustments in budgets. Unless you find new funding, someone will have to give up some budget. That is never easy and you can expect resistance. If it was important enough to make it into your strategic plan, it is important enough to fund it properly. There are some things in every organization that you can stop doing and use the resources for more important opportunities. This is where senior management can take the lead in finding that hidden treasure that managers are so good at burying. Making those adjustments sends a very strong message that you are serious about getting these new initiatives done.

Assign up and coming individuals and your strongest team members to the new strategic initiatives. Again, this sends a clear message of how important the initiative is to the organization. Many organizations will assign a new initiative to someone that is clearly out of favour with senior management. Everyone immediately knows how important it is and that person will get zero support. As a leader, everyone is watching you all the time. Make sure you are sending the right messages.

The strategic plan has set out the most important things for your organization moving forward. These are obvious things to centre your communication plan around. Constant updates and very public celebrations of milestones will keep everyone in the organization focussed and pushing for the success of their piece of the plan. Senior management should never miss an opportunity to talk about the plan and how it is going.

During the plan-to-implement discussion it may be necessary to delay some actions by a few months or longer to deal with higher priorities, resource issues or restructuring. Keep the actions in the draft document so they are not lost. Good ideas will always find their time to be successfully implemented.

Simplicity Keys

➢ Remember that support for the plan must start at the top—ensure and demonstrate leadership buy in
➢ Test the draft plan against the reality of implementation—expect it to be adjusted
➢ Time for sober second thoughts—push for clarity in strategy and action statements
➢ Review feedback from stakeholders and reconnect with them—build support for the plan at the start and at every step
➢ Embrace skeptics
➢ Make sure each person assigned a task knows what is expected—accountability can be scary but must be visible and real
➢ Link rewards directly to achievements of strategy and action items—make celebrating success part of your culture
➢ Stay focussed on the plan even during the latest crisis—use your outside facilitator to ensure constant focus
➢ Ensure proper funding—if something is important enough to put in the plan it is important enough to merit resources
➢ Assign your strongest team members to new initiatives
➢ Build the communication plan around your strategic initiatives

CHAPTER 18

Change

"Organizations do not change, people change"
—Brian J. Rhiness

Much of the discussion in the Plan to Implement was about change. Any strategic plan will involve some amount of change for the organization. It may be small changes or major realignments that shake the organization to the core. Managing change is the single highest hurdle any organization will face and is the number one reason that strategic plans and organizations fail.

No one likes change

We have all encountered people that profess to like change. They like it until it affects them. You can expect that you will run into resistance to your strategic plan because it will mean change from someone. *Change is very personal.* If you forget that, you will not successfully implement your plan.

Many believe that they can change the organization with great ideas or their strong will. They will fail. Organizations do not change. People within that organization may change but only if they have a very good reason to change. We are all looking for the answer to *"what is in it for me?"* when we are facing change. If there is no answer or the answer is not better than the status quo we will dig in and fight any change. Even a minor change of direction or priorities for the organization can mean substantial change to someone's career, work unit, salary or reputation. Egos are at stake here.

Recognize the need to plan for change at the very start of your planning process—the Plan to Plan. We have covered many of the steps that will help you to help others through this change. First, always remember people. In stakeholder engagement we covered how to get people involved. Involving people from the start is absolutely critical to their support for the plan and the necessary changes later. If you take the D.A.D approach, Decide, Announce, Defend, your plan will fail. It is shocking how many organizations still attempt this approach with predictable results. If people feel they have been part of the process and have been heard, there is a much better chance of getting their support, even if they are still skeptical.

Why won't people just accept your great plan?

The Iceberg

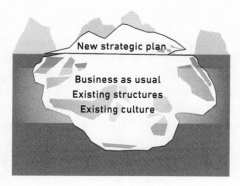

Your great new strategic plan is only the tip of the iceberg. Under the surface is the real danger. The strong desire to carry on business as usual is the safe place for everyone. We are comfortable there. Our existing structures also provide us with comfort and safety. Even if you are not a big fan of your supervisor, you might end up with someone worse. You also have the existing culture of the organization. Changing culture takes time, patience and more time. A great strategic plan when faced with culture, structures and the need for safety and comfort will lose every single time.

All is not lost. Many organizations safely navigate the dangerous waters of change without ending up like the Titanic. The secret is to plan for the iceberg.

We have touched on the preparation for the iceberg throughout the book. If you go back and review the chapters you will see the how tos in every section. Be keenly aware of what you will be facing at the execution stage and you will take the necessary provisions along the way. At each step of the *Strategic Thinking Simplicity* model ask yourself if you are considering all of the iceberg issues. We have mentioned skeptics before and how they are your best friends. Respecting and utilizing skeptics at each step will pay dividends at execution. They will have uncovered most of your soft spots before you get here.

Why do people act this way?

When faced with any change or crisis in our lives we react very predictably. Our reactions follow a pattern summarized in research by Elisabeth Kubler-Ross in the late 1960s. She identified the five stages of grief as: denial, anger, bargaining, depression and acceptance. This predictable reaction can be applied to anything that confronts us in life. We face health issues, relationships end and friends and family members pass away. All of these stresses in life cause us to react. That reaction goes through a series of predictable phases that form a curve. A good friend, the late Stephen Haines from the Haines Centre for Strategic Management compared that curve to a rollercoaster. In many respects it is because we can go down then up and even backwards on the same issue. The curve can repeat itself. Unlike a rollercoaster when you go down one side you do not necessarily go up the other side. The challenge for anyone introducing change is to create the right environment to help people recognize that they will go down one side and there is something to look forward to as they go up the other side of the curve. Turn it into a predictable and safe ride.

We have tried to simplify the curve.

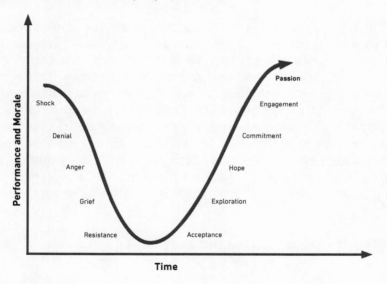

As the graphic illustrates, the first thing that people experience when facing change in their life or work is shock. They then move through denial, anger, grief and resistance. We have all experienced these feelings and they are very real. As we go through each of these phases our performance and morale drops dramatically.

Most people, after maybe being stuck at the bottom for a short while, will move to acceptance (it is not as bad as we thought), exploration (what does this really mean for me?), hope (this could be better) and on to commitment, engagement and passion for the new direction.

Every organization has the early adopters, those that follow the lead, skeptics and cynics. Each of these personality types will go through the cycle in a totally different way. The role of the manager is to recognize each individual, how they react and to provide the support that matches the person. This is similar to helping someone through a personal crisis. Provide the support that meets the needs of that individual.

- The **early adopters** will jump on the new ideas and be over at commitment, engagement and passion before you know it. Harness their enthusiasm to assist others to understand and move forward.
- The **followers** will relatively quickly grasp what the change means to them and start into acceptance and exploration. Be ready to answer lots of questions and communicate constantly. Since they will make up the majority of the people affected, you will need to commit serious time and energy to them.
- The **skeptics** will take a little longer going through the bottom of the curve. Some may even get stuck there for a while. They will need more convincing and will ask much tougher questions. As we have said many times, they are your best friends so listen to them. They will uncover problems and flaws in your plans that you missed. Show everyone that you are listening by being open to comments and suggestions.
- Finally you have the **cynics**. They think this is all bad and nothing you say or do will convince them otherwise. Some cynics will eventually come on side but will never move much past acceptance.

We have all worked with cynics and they suck the life out of organizations. For those that get stuck in the bottom of the curve and refuse to move up the other side, it is probably time to have a conversation about their future with the organization.

When you roll out your new strategic plan these are the predictable reactions. Each person will view it differently and set out on their own individual change curve response. Remember this is not the organization's response. There will literally be a curve for each person in the organization. The organization may feel the effects of all of these curves through decreased productivity, increased sick leave and a drop in sales. In many cases you can feel the morale plummeting. If you have not planned for the roll out of the new strategic plan and the change it brings the entire organization can get stuck at the bottom of the curve and bounce back and forth between resistance and acceptance. That can be a fatal place for any organization. We all know of organizations that have failed as a result.

This is what is really happening in your organization.

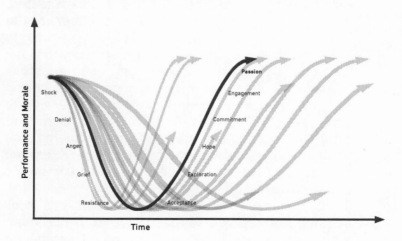

Everyone will be on their own curve with different timelines, trajectories and potential end points. Multiply the number of people in your organization by the number of possibilities and you see what is really going on. To add to the complications, each individual may be on more than one curve at a time. They not only have changes at work but may be facing challenges in their personal life. They will be at different places on each of those curves and it will affect how they react to the new strategic plan. That person that is normally an early adopter and you were expecting to help others through the process is suddenly a cynic. They are probably facing multiple curves and are overwhelmed with all of the change confronting them. As leaders we need to be aware of these realities and provide the extra understanding and support that people need.

It is very common for senior management to struggle with understanding why people "just don't get this". This is particularly evident in our D.A.D. events. Senior management may have spent months discussing the future and how to get there and have thought through all of the possible strategies to move forward. Once they have decided, it is time to tell the world. They have gone through the curve and have come up the other side to engagement and passion. They fail to recognize that the rest of the organization and stakeholders are just hearing this and are starting down through shock and denial.

By involving all stakeholders in the conversation as early as possible you will help the majority of people get through the change cycle quickly and successfully. Remember that real change takes time. The greater the change needed, the longer the time. It may take years to fully implement the desired changes. The continued focus by senior management on where the organization and individuals are is vital.

Go back to the Plan to Plan chapter and consider ways to bring stakeholders into the conversation right at the start.

Simplicity Keys

> Remember that no one likes change—it is personal and distressing
> Avoid the D.A.D. (Decide, Announce, Defend) approach to change—involve everyone in the conversation early and often
> Plan for the iceberg
> Harness early adopters to assist others
> Know that senior management may be at a different place on the curve than everyone else
> Embrace skeptics
> Recall that response to change is predictable, but everyone reacts differently to change and follows their own curve

CHAPTER 19

Action Summary

"I never worry about action, but only inaction"
—Winston Churchill

A strategic plan sitting on the shelf is a waste of time and money. It sucks the life out of people and organizations. Inaction on strategic priorities is the beginning of the end for any organization. Those skeptics that did not believe you were serious about changing things have been proven right. Good luck getting them on side in the future. The iceberg has claimed another victim.

The alternative is senior management clearly focussed on the plan, supporting individuals and their initiatives and celebrating the successes. How do we keep senior managers focussed when they are so easily distracted? With one simple, clear document where they can see at a glance exactly what is happening with all of the strategic priorities.

We strongly recommend recording all strategies and actions in an Action Summary document. This is a living document that will be updated regularly to keep the board and senior management in constant contact with their strategic priorities.

The Action Summary document ties together all of the pieces we discussed in the previous chapters that you will need to keep the organization focussed on strategic priorities.

It includes:

- The Vision, Mission and Core Values
- The strategies and actions from the plan in clear concise wording
- The people that we have assigned and are holding accountable to get each action done
- The timelines to achieve each action
- A status update to ensure things are getting done

You will know very quickly by reviewing this document if the actions have the focus and are getting the support they need. If deadlines are being missed start asking questions. Do the people that have been assigned the actions items have all of the resources they need? Are they getting the support they need?

We use a very simple document with all of the key pieces needed for successful implementation included.

Action Summary Report
Strategic Plan 20XX–20YY

Vision: Updated:

Mission:

Core Values:

Strategies and Actions	Person Responsible	Timeline	Status
Strategy#1			
1.1	1.1	1.1	1.1
1.2	1.2	1.2	1.2
Strategy#2			
2.1	2.1	2.1	2.1
2.2	2.2	2.2	2.2
Strategy#3			
3.1	3.1	3.1	3.1
3.2	3.2	3.2	3.2
Strategy#4			
4.1	4.1	4.1	4.1
4.2	4.2	4.2	4.2
Strategy#5			
5.1	5.1	5.1	5.1
5.2	5.2	5.2	5.2

With a quick glance

The Action Summary includes our Vision, Mission and Core Values to serve as a constant reminder of what is driving us forward.

With a quick glance we can see all of our strategy statements, the actions we are undertaking, who is accountable, the timelines and a status update. The status update can be as simple as icons to indicate: On Time, Ahead of Schedule, Behind Schedule or Completed. You can also include a few words to indicate what is happening with that project or initiative.

We recommend that *every* board meeting and senior executive team meeting start with a review of this document. If these are your most important strategic priorities, what is more important to discuss? This helps everyone stay focussed on what is really important. It also allows everyone to celebrate the successful completion of actions and reward those responsible. If there are problems, immediate steps can be taken to get things back on track.

The Action Summary is the document The Rhiness Group uses in the regular update sessions we hold with clients. It is the foundation of our implementation support guarantee.

As a living document, the Action Summary will constantly be revised. As actions get completed, new actions/next steps will have to be incorporated. It will be easy for the board and management to track progress as revisions happen.

Remember in strategic management that having a plan is only the first step. We need to ensure that budgets, work plans, performance contracts, structures and maybe our culture are adjusted to meet our strategic priorities.

Simple, clear actions and constant focus by everyone in the organization will give you the results you desire. Vision without action is a dream.

Simplicity Keys

> ➤ Action Summary is a one stop collection of all necessary information to ensure everyone stays focused—update it regularly
>
> ➤ Remember that a good Action Summary will allow the board and senior management to see quickly where things are at and ask the right questions
>
> ➤ Remember that these are your strategic priorities—is anything more important?
>
> ➤ Start every board meeting and management team meeting with a review of the Action Summary
>
> ➤ Celebrate successes and milestones
>
> ➤ Respond immediately to get things back on track

CHAPTER 20

Regular Updates

Your strategic plan and the Action Summary are living documents. Just like living things they need to be fed on a regular basis to keep them alive. They are fed by regular attention. By regular, we recommend at least quarterly updates by the board and senior management. If the organization is in significant difficulties the updates should be more often, even weekly if things are critical. This commitment to regular reviews and updates ensures that the strategic plan is being implemented and that the organization is following the strategic management process. Do the strategies and actions have the resources they require? Have budgets been revised? Do performance contracts reflect new responsibilities? Do work unit operating plans support the corporate strategic plan? Tough questions from the board and senior management will keep things on the right track.

In the early life of the strategic plan the quarterly review and update may take a full day. This is time well spent. What is more important to the organization than the strategic priorities that the board and senior management has agreed on? The deeper the understanding is of each initiative and what is happening, the greater their chances of success.

It also provides an excellent opportunity to celebrate the early wins in the strategic plan and demonstrate to the organization that this is real. Each of these updates is an opportunity to communicate what is going on, the successes, the on-going challenges and the commitment to change. Make the updates well publicized events.

We strongly recommend using the outside facilitator that helped you build the plan to lead the regular updates. They will be able to push the group harder and ensure that the process does not turn into a "fill in the blanks exercise". As progress is made on initiatives, the facilitator should be pushing the group to stretch to the next level. The outside facilitator should stay involved until the organization is clearly able to have tough, productive conversations that lead to recognizable changes to the strategic plan and Action Summary documents. Beware of cosmetic changes disguised as execution and strategic management commitment. The facilitator and organization should be pushing each other to greater heights.

Each of the updates should be a real stress test for the strategic plan. They can be treated as a mini strategic planning session. There should be a quick environmental scan done by senior management. Today things are happening very quickly. In all likelihood things are changing daily in your industry. How are those changes affecting your strategic plan? If a strategy is wrong, admit it quickly and fix it immediately.

Stress the plan with questions such as:

- Is the plan working?
- Is each strategy working?
- Are they still the right strategies?
- Are we getting the results we expected?
- What needs to be adjusted or stopped?
- What is missing?
- What has changed in our world?

The first couple of update sessions will be uncomfortable for participants. Tough questions and the associated accountabilities make for long days. Experience has shown us that after that initial discomfort people begin to see the value in these sessions. They actually begin to look forward to them as a place to gain support for their initiatives and to support their colleagues. These quickly turn into powerful team building events. An added bonus for team members is that success in getting your initiatives completed gets you noticed by the board and senior management which is the path to that next promotion.

Announce the update session dates and communicate the results of the sessions immediately afterward. This will reinforce that the process is continuing and everyone is committed to it. Communicating the initiative successes will boost confidence in the plan and the movement forward to your desired future state.

The secret to great execution is *strategic focus and operational flexibility*. This is where you can put that to the test. Can we stay focussed on where we want to be, our Future State, and be nimble enough to adjust to whatever gets in our way of achieving it? You cannot have strategic focus and operational flexibility without regular updates. Looking at your plan once a year or whenever you think of it will result in the plan becoming stale and out-of-date. It will die for lack of regular feeding.

Simplicity Keys

- ➤ Hold at least quarterly updates of the strategic plan for the board and senior management—more often if necessary
- ➤ Announce the update session dates and build communications around the regular updates—people are watching
- ➤ Use your outside facilitator and demand a rigorous review
- ➤ Make an environmental scan update part of the session—things are changing
- ➤ Stress test the plan - if a strategy is not working admit it quickly and fix it immediately
- ➤ Use the update sessions for team building
- ➤ Remember to emphasize strategic focus and operational flexibility

CHAPTER 21

Getting back on track

*"Strategy is good until you get
the first punch in the face"*
—Mike Tyson

Every strategic plan will hit bumps on the road to success. Expect them and plan for them. Use those bumps to re-energize the organization and as another opportunity to communicate your vision, mission, core values and strategic priorities. This is where the board and senior management needs to step up. The CEO is ultimately responsible for the implementation of the strategic plan, so this is a critical leadership point for that individual. All stakeholders are watching and the reaction from the CEO will send an immediate and powerful message to everyone.

Be honest and admit when you are off track.

Remember the iceberg. In spite of the nice new shiny strategic plan, people want to stay in the comfort of existing structures and culture. They want business as usual. If the CEO and senior management do not push, the organization will carry on as if the new plan does not exist. It is the sole responsibility of the CEO and senior management to ensure that the plan moves into the strategic management cycle. They must ask themselves some difficult questions:

- Have you held regular plan update sessions?
- Do stakeholders really understand where you are going?
- Where is the majority of staff on the change curve?
- Have individual work units in the organization adjusted their operating plans to support the new plan?
- Have budgets been adjusted so that the strategic priorities have the resources they need?
- Have performance contracts been updated so that individuals are clear on the results expected of them and what they are being measured on?
- Have organizational structures been adjusted to support the new direction you are taking?
- Are people being rewarded for the new expectations?
- Do you have the commitment and support you need from the board and CEO?

Honest answers to these questions will tell you if you are off track and how far. Finding the answers may require some effort. You will have to ask people in the organization where they are at and actually listen to what they are saying. If they are still in denial, you should not expect passionate commitment to their new tasks. If you have not updated their performance contracts and allowed them to stop doing some things, do not expect them to change their daily routines. They know what they will be measured against and it is already on paper. Your actions will always speak louder than your words. The new strategic plan is only a bunch of words until you put them into action. Remember that as a senior manager you are always being watched.

A common excuse for parking the strategic plan is a sudden crisis. This excuse is used so often that it should be laughable but it is not funny. Many organizations fail or at least fail to meet their full potential because of this lame excuse. This is a not so subtle attempt to carry on business as usual and forget about that new plan. The iceberg strikes again. Every organization faces crises, large or small, constantly. It is a reality. Get over it.

A "crisis" is a perfect opportunity to reinforce the existence and value of the strategic plan. This is the perfect time for the CEO to step up. Hold a special planning meeting to update the strategic plan with the response to the crisis. Assign people accordingly and set aggressive deadlines to resolve the crisis. Stress that all other initiatives in the plan are still on track and communicate the update to all stakeholders. The culture is starting to change.

Being off track can be used as the perfect excuse to re-energize the strategic plan and the organization. Reboot the plan with new communication. Celebrate the things that are on track and the people that have been successful with their initiatives. Announce formal update sessions and the dates so that people know when things are happening and will anticipate further good news stories. Build the trust with all stakeholders that you are back on track and will stay there.

Simplicity Keys

- ➢ Remember that every plan will go off track—plan for it
- ➢ Never forget that the CEO is responsible for implementation of the plan—time to step up
- ➢ Admit when you are off track
- ➢ Remember the iceberg
- ➢ Review the tough questions list
- ➢ Make sure the plan has been incorporated into the strategic management cycle
- ➢ Remember that you are being watched by all stakeholders
- ➢ Use being off track as an opportunity to re-energize the plan—don't let a crisis become the cause to delay or abandon the plan
- ➢ Announce the dates of future update sessions and communicate results immediately after

CHAPTER 22

Scenario Planning

*"They let the shit hit the fan, and
then they made a plan"*
—Jimmy Buffet, "A lot to Drink About"

You are #1 in the world. Your products are known for their quality and safety. People are so addicted to your device it is nicknamed the "crackberry". Your company operates hundreds of highly technical sites around the world. Your revenues are in the billions of dollars selling products the world cannot live without.

You are on the top of the world. What could possibly go wrong?
If you are Toyota, Blackberry or BP—a lot!

You may not operate on the same scale as these three companies but events can be just as damaging to your future. The impact on shareholders, stakeholders, employees, the environment, suppliers, customers and innocent bystanders can range from inconvenient to catastrophic.

Do you really understand the implications of your decisions on your organization? Have you truly considered the various scenarios around those decisions? The quick answer is "of course we have". The newspapers are full of stories to prove that you have not.

We have added this chapter on scenario planning as a bonus, stand alone piece. Scenario planning is an extremely effective tool that can enhance your strategic planning process and the resulting strategic plan. It is near the end of the book because it is an additional layer of rigour in the planning process that may be difficult for an organization to manage. This is of particular concern if you are doing your first strategic plan. We recommend that organizations get a good plan in place, focus on great execution with regular updates and bring scenario planning into their planning process in year two.

The chapter is laid out to match each step in the strategic planning process. When you feel you are ready to use scenario planning, simply add the extra level of rigour to each step in the *Strategic Thinking Simplicity* model. It will take your planning to a much higher level.

Start with a plan

Most organizations recognize the need for crisis plans. These plans are built to respond to such things as natural disasters, terrorism, major staff disruptions, technological breakdowns or a financial crunch. In spite of these being very basic crisis plans, the daily news carries stories of organizations that have not been prepared. In some cases they had a crisis plan on paper, but it was sitting on a shelf and was useless when they needed it.

When a crisis hits, you do not want to start considering options. An immediate, well thought out response, before you need it, can save your company.

Having a crisis response is not enough and it is not the purpose of this chapter. The purpose is to make scenario planning part of your strategic plan.

Every organization needs a strategic plan. If you are trying to get by without one, you will simply not be successful and will fall victim to the inevitable surprises every organization encounters.

You are probably saying that Toyota, Blackberry and BP had strategic plans and look what happened. They did have plans and for the most part those plans were working just fine. What is missing?

First, let's be clear. Toyota is a great company and makes great cars. They earned the reputation they have for quality and safety. BP did not get to the heights they have by being ineffective and reckless. We still have Blackberry's and we love them.

In all three cases, the companies suffered from the common phenomenon of believing in their own invincibility and the arrogance that accompanies it. Success can make you blind to your weaknesses. If you do not stay humble as an organization and as leaders, the world will quickly remind you. The financial crisis humbled many an infallible manager.

We can't plan for everything

Accidents happen. It's absolutely true that we can't plan for everything. We are not very good at predicting unlikely events. For an excellent book, check out The Black Swan by Nassim Nicholas Taleb. A better approach is to focus on the *consequences* of any extreme events. This approach allows for the development of strategies to withstand or avoid any impacts.

By adding a rigorous scenario planning process to your strategic planning you can ensure you know and understand as many potential outcomes as possible.

Could BP have foreseen the possibility of an explosion and oil leaking into the ocean? Of course. Was it likely to happen? No, there are thousands of wells operating successfully around the world. Those successes led to some fatally bad decisions.

The most critical question in your strategic planning, scenario planning and day-to-day operations must be: *"What if?"*

Remember that these processes must be led by the board and senior management. If they are not engaged in asking the tough questions, do not expect anyone else in the organization to do it.

Many articles and case studies have been written about the BP disaster in the Gulf of Mexico. The bottom line in most reviews is that they dropped the ball on a number of decision points. In each of those cases a simple *"What if?"* would have helped. For example: *"What if?"* our efforts to cut costs on a drilling rig leads to a leak? What would be the impact? These very basic questions likely were never asked. If they were considered, and the answer was *"it is a risk we are willing to take,"* that leads to another set of very serious legal and ethical questions that will be asked.

From reports on the spill, it appears that safety violations and other technical concerns were well known, but not to senior management. If true this would be an extreme example of senior management not wanting to know and not asking key questions. The end result was a choice made between short term cost savings and the health of the organization.

There was a report of a Toyota executive e-mail claiming credit for saving millions by not moving to correct the faulty gas pedal. They saved millions to lose billions in both dollars and reputation. Is your organization being penny wise and dollar foolish?

We don't need negative scenarios

Optimism is important and must be the foundation of any strategic plan. This chapter advocates a balance between optimism, realism and pessimism. Most organizations (and individuals) are afraid to talk about what can go wrong because they fear appearing negative. If your company is announcing a major merger, it is not wise to suggest publicly that the synergies expected are unlikely to work out. In fact, in 75% of mergers the synergies do not work out as expected. Before making the announcement, a great *"What if?"* would be: *"What if?"* we do not get the estimated 25% synergy saving as expected? Does the merger still make sense? If the answer is yes, then go for it.

> *In scenario planning, optimism is great—but*
> *it is even better if combined with a splash*
> *of realism and a dash of pessimism.*
> —Brian J. Rhiness

The law of expected surprises

A common trap for managers is the belief they can rely on managing their way through any unforeseen problems. They may get through it, but at what cost to the organization? They may also face multiple surprises at the same time, which compounds the problem. Recent examples show that the firm may survive, but responsible managers do not. Most managers will claim they want no surprises, but do not create an environment that keeps unexpected surprises to a minimum.

A robust scenario planning process implemented with strategic planning will greatly reduce the number of unforeseen problems. We want only **expected surprises**. These are events that we acknowledge *can happen*, and that we can clearly answer what we are doing throughout the organization *to ensure they do not happen.*

As a car manufacturer you can expect that you will have recalls. What are you doing at every level of the organization to ensure that it will not happen or to minimize the impact? It needs to become a **cultural response**. Implement the law of expected surprises in your organization.

If you are pumping oil from deep in the ocean, an *expected surprise* would be a leak. Had BP senior management considered a worst case scenario—an unstoppable leak—they may not have chosen the cheapest route as the course. They also would have had a crisis response ready to go that would have focussed on such things as quickly stopping the leak, rapid clean up and how to effectively respond to the media circus. Why did we need this crisis to *start* talking about how to both stop such a leak and clean it up? A small amount of critical foresight will reduce a large amount of hindsight.

"What if" we had a gusher?

Watch for signals. BP apparently had hundreds of safety violations, while their competitors had few. That is a big, red flag *"What if?"* question for the board and senior managers. What if those violations are a sign of bigger culture and management issues?

There are at least one dozen major factory fires in the world every single day. Do you know where your suppliers' supplies come from? How might a fire, tsunami or earthquake affect you?

Implement a law of expected surprises *at every level* of your organization. Ask the tough questions inside your organization, and avoid doing it in front of television cameras.

Encourage and embrace skeptics throughout the organization to improve the quality of discussions and decisions. Skeptics are your best friends because they do not get caught up in the "group think" and "go along to get along" diseases that infect many organizations.

In many cases you will need outside help to shift the culture and provide a safe environment for free flowing discussions that will implement the law of expected surprises throughout your organization. This law must be implemented first at the board and senior management team level. It sends a powerful message to all staff and partner organizations.

Scenario planning in action

We are ready to do scenario planning and enforce the Law of Expected Surprises. Where do we start? Start with a good strategic planning process. Scenario planning without a strategic plan is a waste of time. We recommend the *Strategic Thinking Simplicity* platform for your planning process. It is based on systems thinking which leading organizations have found to be the most effective foundation for results based planning.

Strategic Thinking Simplicity model

At each step of the *Strategic Thinking Simplicity* model you can dramatically increase your results by adding scenario based questions to the conversation. Here's how it works:

Future Environmental Scan

The environmental scan provides the first opportunity to review all things that could affect the organization, positively or negatively, in the future. Remember to involve as many staff, stakeholders and partners as practical in the process. People support what they help create, and you can get valuable insights from interested parties outside your normal comfort zone.

Look at the future trends, projections, opportunities and risks that face you in the coming years in the following areas:

- Industry
- Stakeholders
- Political/Regulatory
- Organization
- Customers
- Competition
- Technology
- Financial
- Natural
- Social
- Reputation
- Others

The key questions you must ask are: *What* is the trend? *So what* does that mean to our organization? *Now what* do we need to do to prepare for it?

This is your first, and best, place to get a head start on potential issues. Do not settle for data, general surveys and generic reports—dig deep! Push the discussion outside the comfort zones. We can only speculate on how much different Blackberry would look today if they had entertained a more open, honest and visionary discussion of their customer's future needs, technology direction and the competition. The information and opinions were out there—it appears they made a deliberate decision not to look or to ignore them. Does your organization have any signs of institutional blindness?

Do not be constrained by the environmental scan. Use it as a time to ask *"What if?"* for both challenges and opportunities. Turn challenges on their head and ask how they can be turned into opportunities, new products or new lines of business.

The environmental scan must be an *ongoing process*. All staff must be focussed on the industry, competitors, customers and anything that may affect the organization. They are your very best early warning system. Waiting until next year's update will be too late. Never farm the environmental scan out to an outside agency. No one knows your organization, your industry or your potential opportunities better than your own people. It can however be very beneficial to bring in some outside facilitation and experts to push your thinking to the necessary discomfort levels.

Future state

The future state place in the *Strategic Thinking Simplicity* model is where we really start planning by establishing our desired outcomes. What is our vision for the future of the organization? What is our mission and what core values differentiate us?

We strongly encourage organizations to get a *"Helicopter View"* of the situation at this stage. Detach yourself from daily circumstances and look from 10,000 feet, at what is really going on around you.

The need for well defined and clear desired outcomes demands each proposed outcome be tested against all known and potential surprises. Optimism needs to be balanced with some really blunt *"What ifs?* If the proposed outcome passes the toughest "What *ifs?"* you have a winner. Resist the temptation to fall back on general statements to avoid difficult discussions. "We will grow market share" is not an outcome, it is a cop out. This is an ideal place to have team members take turns acting as skeptics. Keep at it until you have a simple, clear outcome statement that can be easily communicated and understood.

Success measures

How will we know when we get there? A dynamic measurement system is vital. Direct linkage to the outcomes ensures that we continue to measure the right things. Again, we must ask: *"What if?"* something changes? Are we still measuring the right things? What gets measured gets done, so make sure it is the right measure.

Current state

In the current state assessment, we are looking at our organization as it sits today. What resources, structures and cultures exist? A key question at this stage is: *"What if"* the current structures, culture and resources cannot (or will not) support the desired outcomes?

This is the major reason that change initiatives and strategic plans fail. Many organizations do not seriously consider the cultural and structural barriers that exist in their organizations. Nowhere in the strategic planning process are skeptics more important than here. There are an unlimited number of *"What if?"* questions that must be asked and answered at this stage. Do not attempt to skip over the tough discussions and decisions.

It is difficult for organizations to be constructively critical of their current state. A lot of egos, budgets, bonuses and careers are involved. It is vital for leaders to show the way and put everything (including their egos) on the table.

Action Bridge

The final step in the *Strategic Thinking Simplicity* model is the Action Bridge. From previous steps we know where we want to be and where we are today. The action bridge provides the core strategies and actions that fill the gap between the current state and the desired outcomes (the future).

The strategies really answer the question, "How do we get there from here?" Strategies provide the clarity of direction and the activities to move the team to action. Ensure your strategy statements are clear and concise—one sentence. We like to start this sentence with "We will . . . ." It is an action statement. The action points under each strategy statement also need to be very specific. These will be the projects, programs, initiatives and steps taken by the organization to successfully completed the strategy and move us toward our desired outcomes. These actions will be given to individuals so clarity is vital. Also, they must be linked to those individual's performance contracts. This is where we build the implementation phase from. It is also where the rubber really hits the road. An effective strategic plan is 20% planning and 80% execution. A great plan with poor execution is a failure.

Contingency plans

In planning, the words *"scenario"* and *"contingency"* are many times used interchangeably. Your organization may already have contingency plans. Don't confuse the terms. *You need both.* Start with a review of potential scenarios, and then build contingencies to address key problem areas. If you have only one supplier of a key component, a possible scenario would be that the supply is interrupted for any reason. The contingency would be to find an alternate supply source—*before* you need it.

Rigorous scenario review

If the organization structures and culture clash with the plan, the plan will lose every time. A common problem for organizations, especially if they are in trouble, is to have an extremely ambitious list of activities for the first year of the new plan. They forget that they have ongoing activities, set structures and possibly a culture resistant to change.

At this stage, a very rigorous scenario review is essential. All strategies must be tested against known factors and potential *"expected surprises"*. We are building strategies that are flexible enough to adjust quickly to unknown forces. The team needs to dig deep with *"What if?"* questions.

Scenario planning should be part of the conversation at every regular update session. It is that extra level of rigour against which every new strategy and action is tested.

Summary

The rigorous use of *"What if?"* at all parts of the *Strategic Thinking Simplicity* process is the most effective way of improving your organization's chances of success.

As leaders we need to call "STOP" at all stages of the planning process and encourage *"What if?"* conversations. We need to test the thinking and prevent groupthink, extreme optimism and unrealistic expectations. This may initially increase the overall planning time, but it is time well spent. Once it becomes part of the ongoing planning process it will save time and dramatically improve results.

Strategic planning has been given a bad rap because of the high incidence of failures. There are too many ill thought out strategies and actions. We can improve the success rate by adding rigorous scenario planning to the process.

Unleash the power of scenario planning in your organization.

Simplicity Keys

> Unleash the power of scenario planning in your organization
> Implement the law of expected surprises
> Never forget that success can blind you to your weaknesses
> Ask yourself whether your organization has institutional blindness
> Ask "What if?"—focus on the consequences of an extreme event
> Asking tough questions starts at the board and senior management
> Bring in outside help to guide scenario planning and help shift culture
> Add scenario planning rigour to each part of the Strategic Thinking Simplicity model
> Use environmental scanning as an early warning system

CHAPTER 23

Continuous Learning

"Leadership and learning are
indispensible to each other"
John F. Kennedy

This final chapter is not a summary or an ending. It is a challenge to use this book as a beginning, to use strategic planning to stretch yourself and your organization to greater heights.

Leadership is about continuous learning and helping others achieve all that they can. One of the most important roles of a leader is to help set the strategic direction of their organization and ensure that it is successfully implemented. A simple, clear plan that has been developed by all of the key stakeholders dramatically improves the chances of success.

A strategic plan is much more than a document. Strategic planning is a living process that must be supported with regular nourishment. A plan must be incorporated into a strategic management cycle and be the constant focus of the board of directors and management teams. Every board and management meeting should begin with a review of the strategic priorities and a status update.

The Action Summary Report makes that update quick and simple. The conversations that it will generate will become the new fuel to grow the organization.

The strategic management cycle requires that new strategic priorities be supported in budgets, individual performance contracts and work unit operating plans. This means some difficult decisions must be made. Support from senior management will be absolutely necessary if the new strategies and actions are to be successfully completed. Everyone in the organization must be held truly accountable for their role in getting the job done.

On at least a quarterly basis the strategic plan should receive a more rigorous and formal review by the board and senior management. The entire organization should be aware of this regular focus being paid to the plan. If the leadership is focussed on it and holding themselves accountable, that focus will spread throughout the organization. The greatest danger to a great strategic plan is to be left sitting on the shelf. There will be a great many excuses used to derail your plan. If your employees do not believe that senior management is totally dedicated to the plan then the first crisis will be enough to totally derail it. If there is not a legitimate crisis, someone will make one up.

A new plan means change and no one likes change. Be on constant lookout for those that would derail it. A real crisis is a great opportunity to demonstrate the power of your strategic plan. Use the crisis to update the plan with the crisis response, while at the same time reaffirming the support for the strategic priorities. This will ensure the strategic focus and operational flexibility that is the secret to success.

The same principles apply when building your personal life plan. The plan needs regular nourishment, updating and your continual focus. Do not let the first crisis derail your plan. Make some specific adjustments and recommit to the plan.

Commit yourself and your organization to continuous learning. The Simplicity Keys section at the end of this chapter gives a few examples of the great resources that are out there to assist you in your journey. These books by great authors and others too many to list will provide you with unlimited knowledge and motivation.

A good strategic plan should make you uncomfortable. The plan is about choices and tough decisions and those will be difficult. If you are comfortable with the plan it is not stretching you or the organization and you are going nowhere.

A good strategic plan is about bringing strength and focus to the things that really matter to you and your organization. Strategy is personal. Own the plan.

Simplicity—Clarity—Action—Results

Simplicity Keys

- Strategic and Systems Thinking—Stephen Haines
- The 7 Habits of Highly Effective People—Stephen Covey
- The Fifth Discipline Fieldbook—Peter Senge
- The Black Swan—Nassim Nicholas Taleb
- The Tipping Point—Malcolm Gladwell
- Get Me Off The Treadmill—Valerie F. MacLeod
- How the Mighty Fall—Jim Collins
- Managers, not MBAs—Henry Mintzberg
- Strategic Project Management made Simple—Terry Schmidt
- Awesomely Simple—John Spence
- Good Strategy, Bad Strategy—Gordon Rumelt
- Execution—Larry Bossidy and Ram Charan
- Systems Thinking The New Frontier—Stephen Haines
- Billion Dollar Lessons—Paul Carroll and Chunka Mui
- The Power of a Positive No—William Ury
- Winning—Jack Welch
- Competitive Strategy—Michael E. Porter

ACKNOWLEDGMENTS

There are many people to thank for supporting the development of a book. Some of those people have provided that support over many years. My family and the many colleagues have provided important feedback and mentoring, even when I did not want it. They had the patience to allow me to make the mistakes that learning and growth requires. I learned much from them by asking endless questions but most importantly by shutting up and watching them. The book covers core values which are undoubtedly the most important factor in leadership and life. I have benefited from be associated with many people of the very best character and values.

Thank you to Michael Flood and Michael Rhiness for help on the editing and refining of terminology to get the simplicity and clarity we are seeking. Justin Pritchard did a great job on graphics and cover design. A number of my global associates gave feedback on concepts, designs and terminology and their continuing guidenance and support is greatly appreciated.

I would also like to thank my many clients for their support and patience as we tested new ideas and approaches. As expected, not every idea is a good one and their feedback was invaluable in building a better product.

As special thanks goes to my friend the late Stephen Haines. Steve had a great passion for systems thinking and assisting others in achieving desired results. He is an inspiration and is missed.

Thank you to the folks at Trafford Publishing for making the publishing process not only simple but easy. Special thanks to Earl Thomas and Lou Fuentes.

DEFINITIONS

These definitions are provided to support the discussion in the book and may or may not match common dictionary definitions.

Accountability—answerable for results. This requires clarity of direction and specifying who is answerable for what.

Actions—these are the specific projects, initiatives and programs undertaken to ensure the success of each strategy.

Action Bridge—the strategies and actions that take us from our current state to our desired future state.

Action Summary—a powerful tool used in executing the strategic plan. The document contains a summary of all strategies, actions, project leads, timelines and status updates. It is essential to support accountability.

Change—to transform, transfer or convert. Strategic planning will always involve change and will be difficult.

Change Curve—the predictable phases that people go through when facing change or stress.

Core Values—how we act, or should act, while fulfilling our mission and achieving our vision.

Current State—where you and your organization are today. An honest review of your current state is critical before moving forward to your desired future state.

Cynics—someone who continually expresses a bitter or disinterested attitude. They are not helpful to the strategic planning process or the organization.

D.A.D.—decide, announce, defend. This is an outdated and ineffective approach to planning and change.

Desired Outcomes—what we want out of the planning process. Can also be referred to as the end state, objectives, goals or where do we want to end up. They are included in the future state discussion and can also be helpful in project planning.

Engagement—having people involved and committed.

Environment—the world where we operate on a daily basis.

Environmental scan—a necessary step at the beginning of the planning process. The scan assesses your world today and in the future across a wide range of areas critical to you and your organization. It will help you identify "Black Swans" (improbable events that have very great impact).

Execution—putting your strategic plan to work. The most difficult part of strategic planning and where most plans fail. Without execution the strategic plan becomes a document setting on the shelf collecting dust. It can also be referred to as implementation.

Facilitator—a person brought in from outside the organization to guide the conversation and process.

Future State—where we want to end up. The future state includes the vision, mission and core values.

Goals—see desired outcomes

Helicopter view—taking a higher level view of what is going on. This helps support strategic thinking and focus on the desired outcomes.

Implementation—putting your strategic plan to work. It can also be referred to as execution.

Lagging Indicators—part of the measures of success. They are historical, quantifiable results at the end of a period.

Leader—the person responsible for setting the strategic direction for a group and ensuring execution. This individual is also responsible for developing people and processes for a successful organization.

Leading Indicators—part of the measures of success. They are predictive, processes, activities and behaviours. They do not have to be numbers.

Life plan—your personal strategic plan for the future.

Measures—see success measures.

Mission—your unique purpose. This will answer the questions: Why do we exist? What business are we in? What do we produce or provide? Who do we serve?

Outcomes—results achieved.

Outputs—the amount produced; production.

Plan to Implement—a critical step after the development of a draft strategic plan. This is the official beginning of the execution phase.

Plan to Plan—a critical step before the planning process begins. This step ensures that everyone has a shared understanding of the desired outcomes of the planning process and all details.

Planning Retreat—a scheduled event dedicated to strategic planning.

Resources—the people, facilities, funds, technology and processes available in implement the strategic plan.

Scenario Planning—understanding all possible events and their implications for you and your organization.

Skeptic—someone that asks tough questions about your plan. These people are your best friends.

Stakeholders—anyone that can affect the success of your strategic plan. These are important people to have involved in the planning process from the beginning.

Strategic Focus and Operational Flexibility—a fundamental principle of maintaining focus on where you want to end up and the flexibility to adjust strategies and actions quickly to ensure you get there.

Strategic Leadership—providing the vision and direction for the success of an organization. This must be supported with the ability to engage others and implement change.

Strategic Management—all of the pieces required for success. The strategic management cycle model ensures continual focus on the pieces and their linkage.

Strategic Thinking—an unwavering focus on the desired outcomes of your business, project or initiative.

Strategic Plan—the final approved living process. It is much more than a document.

Strategic Planning—an ongoing process of discussion, focus and renewal.

Strategic Thinking Simplicity—a simple planning model.

Strategies—the "how tos" that will bridge the gap from the current state to the desired future state.

Success Measures—how we ensure we are moving in the right direction. Feedback is one of the cornerstones of systems thinking.

SWOT—a tool used in assessing the current state. Engages a deep conversation on issues internal to the organization (Strengths and Weaknesses) and external to the organization (Opportunities and Threats).

Systems Thinking—a holistic approach that views the whole as being primary and the parts as secondary. This is the foundation of effective strategic planning.

The Law of Expected Surprises—something every organization should implement. This law can be supported by rigours scenario planning.

Values—see core values.

Vision—what our ideal future looks like. A vision is absolutely critical for success.

INDEX